It's Impossible Until You Do It

Succeeding In The Face of Adversity

Written by Tim Conners

Edited by Eliza McGowen

Copyright © 2016 by Timothy Conners

Printed in the United States of America by
Timothy Conners and Tim Possible Publishing

First Printing, 2016

ISBN 978-0-692-82053-7

Tim Possible, LLC

www.MounTimPossible.com

Dedication

To Erik Weihenmayer. There were many people involved in saving my life, but without you in it I never would have started living again. You are my friend, you are my mentor, and you are my hero. You also were the light in my life when I needed it most. I will never be able to thank you enough for teaching me it doesn't take sight to have vision.

Acknowledgements

To my Mother and Father. I don't even know where to start. Throughout my childhood you taught me how to do the right thing, how to be a member of a community and team, and how to never give up. These values ended up playing a significant role in saving my life, but I couldn't have survived without your love. You gave up everything in your lives to make sure I lived, and you also brought me up when I didn't always have the strength to do it on my own. Moving forward in the future I know sometimes you have your doubts, but I know no one believes in me more than you two, and no matter what happens in our lives I will never be able to thank you enough for everything you have done.

To my brother Michael. We fight a lot, we disagree even more, but at the end of the day we love each other. It is because of your sacrifice to be my bone marrow donor that I am still here today, and although I try, I don't think I will ever be able to repay you for saving my life. I know you will go on to be a great father in the next chapter of your life, and I look forward to being a part of that.

To my Grandma Esther and Grandma Norma. You are the people on the other end of the phone when I need to vent. You are the people who hold me to high standards including calling you every Sunday. And you are the loving overbearing grandparents who have spoiled me throughout my entire life. I love you both so much, and I am blessed to have you in my life.

To my family. I couldn't ask for more. You have been right by my side my entire life, and stepped away from your own lives when I was sick to provide me with the strength, love, and support I needed to survive. You all are special in your individual ways, and even now you find ways to still take time out of your own lives to help me in my mission to help others. I can't thank you enough, and I am blessed to have a family like you.

To my close friends who are just another part of my family. You know who you are, and I love you. You make me laugh, you make me smile, and you have my back whenever I need it most. Without all of you in my life I wouldn't get the enjoyment or experience the success that I do, and that is why although we might not share the same blood, I love you all as if you were my blood relatives.

To my doctors. Some of you have saved my life, some of you have helped me deal with the side effects of my treatments, and some of you have helped me with the things that seem small in comparison like the sinus infections I seem to get every year, but all of you have given me the opportunity to live a healthy life. I couldn't thank all of you enough, and it is because people like you do the work that you do that people like me are able to change the world.

To my teachers, coaches, and mentors. Before I became sick you guided me to reach the high levels of success I was capable of. After getting sick you worked with me so I could become strong enough to start succeeding in my life again. And now you help me take my life experience so I can share it with the world and make it a better place. I am a culmination of everything you have taught me, and you will always be some of the most important people in my life.

To my community of Fulton New York. An individual is only as strong as the people they surround themselves with, and we may be an odd bunch, but I wouldn't trust any other community in the world with my life. You were there when I needed it, and I will never be able to repay you for the love, support, and prayers you provided me with to survive.

To everyone who helped me in bringing this book into a reality. It wasn't easy, we worked on a short time line towards the end, but together we did it. Whatever success comes from this book is yours as well, and you exemplify what is possible when you surround yourself with amazing people.

To everyone who has helped me in my life achieve success in the face of my adversity. I don't know if I will ever be able to properly acknowledge all of you the way you deserve, but know there are so many of you that have made a huge difference in my life, and I will never forget that as long as I live.

Table of Contents

Dedication Page

Acknowledgements Page

Table of Contents Page

Introduction

My name is Tim Conners, and it is officially time for us to live life fully, make a difference, and redefine possible together! As America's Ambassador of Hope, I wake up each day with a purpose. That purpose is to help others get the most that they can out of their lives despite their circumstances. Having been there myself, I know what it is like to be completely overwhelmed with the unexpected twists and turns life can throw our way, but through overcoming the barriers in my life, I have learned what it means to be successful in the face of that adversity.

At only 15 years old, my life would change forever. I would go from an athletic, able-bodied freshman in high school to, in less than 6 months, a blind Leukemia patient in the intensive care unit at Boston Children's hospital whose parents just learned they should prepare for their last good byes because I wasn't going to make it. I know my experience may be extreme, but I'm sure that I am not the only one who has experienced things in their life where they felt completely out of control, and as a result, lost hope. Although I don't remember lying there in that hospital bed, I do consider it one of the darkest moments in my life. What I won't forget, though, are all of the hardships I have faced since.

It was anything but easy—there were a lot of tears shed along the way—and I would need to grow up at a very young age, but in the face of my mortality I would learn so much when it came to being successful. These life lessons have propelled me forward in my mission of living life fully, and have allowed me to experience success on many different levels. Academically, I am finishing my senior year at Ithaca College in New York State where I will graduate with a Bachelor of Arts degree in Communication Studies. Physically, I am hiking mountains and working toward summiting Africa's tallest mountain, Mount Kilimanjaro, in 2017. Most importantly, through my story and the valuable lessons I have learned, I am inspiring others around the globe to achieve their own fulfillment in the face of adversity.

The reason I decided to write this book is because although my speaking career has blessed me with the opportunity to travel around the country to share my message of hope, there are still so many people out there, and you may be one of them, who I haven't been able to reach yet. Having become a voice for those in their life encountering hardship, I want to make sure that people—whether it is another person experiencing a life-threatening illness, whether it is another person learning to live with a disability, or whether it is someone who has gotten to that point where continuing on with life just doesn't seem worth it anymore—that they get the message that in the darkest of moments there is still hope. Also, even if you aren't someone who is at a point in your life where all seems lost, the information in this book can still provide you with the principles to experience success in ways you never could have imagined.

The principles included in this book are a result of the experiences I have had in my life, but I want you to know that these experiences include all the knowledge I have gained from some of the most successful speakers and life coaches in the world. Ranging from Dale Carnegie and his classic *How to Win Friends and Influence People* to Steven Covey and his life changing *7 Habits of Highly Effective People*, I have gained a vast repository of time-tested knowledge that has produced tangible outcomes in my own life. Also, as someone who values his integrity highly and is a man of his word, I wouldn't be writing this book if I didn't feel the lessons I have to teach would help others. I believe this so wholeheartedly that I am willing to put my reputation on the line by saying I promise you that if you take away even one thing from this book you will feel more in control of the outcomes in your life than ever before

Two of the most valuable lessons I have learned in my life are that people don't care how much you know until they know why you care and people don't hear you until they know you. I hope by now you understand that I want you to live the most fulfilling life you possibly can, and I believe everybody has the ability to succeed even if they don't believe it themselves yet. Also, I want to make sure you know who I am before you continue on because you won't take my words to heart until you know how I got here and who I am. So it's time for you to turn the page and hear the story behind how I faced my adversity and became the man I am today.

Chapter 1 The New Normal

It was 2009 when I started off on the biggest journey of my life. I was entering G. Ray Bodley High School in Fulton New York, and like all 15-year old kids I had a lot of things on my mind. Who was I going to sit with at lunch; what were my teachers going to be like; was I finally going to get a girlfriend?

Before I entered the doors of my high school on freshman first day I went through what I thought were the three toughest weeks of my life. I was on the junior varsity football team, and we started double session practices three weeks before school began. Each day our team would set out from the high school to the Cedar Street Practice Field, and by the time the sun was out in full force things really started to get tough. Some of the days were excruciatingly hot and humid in central New York, and just because conditions weren't the best for running around in football equipment didn't mean we didn't practice.

Preseason football pushed me physically and mentally to my limits, but I was determined to try and make it through. Whether it was trying to execute plays perfectly so my coaches didn't yell, or trying to be the fastest in sprints, which was tough because at 215 pounds I didn't have a runner's build, or trying not to get killed by the biggest kids on our team during drills, I somehow got up every morning to go back each day. I picked up some valuable lessons during these three weeks, like don't get on coaches bad side because that meant a long day, and before I knew it I was getting ready for my first day of school and I had survived double sessions.

The first class of the day for me was Spanish, and at the end of my first day was the course that became the bane of my existence: Honors World History. It was the first time this course was being offered in my high school, and as someone who never had to try hard at getting good grades, I had met my match.

Although I managed to complete all of my summer homework for my history course by the first day of class, which consisted of reading two books and posting about them in a blog to share with the other students in the course, things would only get more difficult as the school year continued on. By the end of the first week of classes, unlike in my other courses where we were just meeting our teachers, I was walking out of my honors World History Course having just taken my first test.

I was already frustrated with my History Course, and it hadn't even been a full week of school yet. Even though the test was tough, and I only studied a map for two hours the day before school started, I got a 95 on it. I was mad with the grade because I wanted a 100, but since over 50% of the class failed the exam, I decided I was fine with it.

After a couple weeks into school I had hit a point of real frustration. Football was really taking its toll on me. Although a lot of people would have been happy to be me because I was starting on both sides of the ball as a freshman, I let the pressure get to me. I was paranoid I would make a mistake, or worse, make a fool of myself, and when I thought about letting my entire team down I made myself sick. Thankfully, once I got into a game I was fine, but the moments leading up to them were some of the worst of my life, and in those moments I would have done anything not to play.

Football was tough, but I was used to this pressure I placed on myself from sports. The real kicker for me was that I was doing poorly in my Honors World History Course, because I never struggled academically. I wasn't the only one doing badly, but I wasn't used to ever doing worse than an A. I didn't care that this was supposed to be the stuff I would need to do to pass the AP World History Exam to get college credit.

I was beside myself. When I would get failing grades back on quizzes and tests, even though I wasn't doing the readings, it pushed me over the edge. I blamed my teacher for my lackluster performance.

My teacher had the patience and strength to put up with me and all of my excuses, and by the end of my first football season she had won over my heart. I am not sure if it was the day that she worked with me after school to study for an exam, and then actually walked with me to football practice that afternoon, or the fact that she continually pointed out the positives in me and my work, but Sue Dauphin was a true mentor in my life, and she brought out the best in me.

It seemed like I had just gotten control of my life with all the ins and outs of high school, but then a day I had been avoiding since the end of the last sports season came. It was wrestling season again.

For some background, Fulton always seemed to rally the most behind two sports. The first was football, and a Friday night meant packed bleachers and a lot of Raider pride, but if football was big in my community then wrestling was gigantic. The worst part of it all was my dad was the varsity coach of both. Although my connection to football with my father never seemed to weigh on me too much, something about wrestling brought the worst out in me. It didn't help that my father was a two-time All-American and a one-time Division Three national champ, as well as one of the best coaches in New York State with multiple state championship teams under his belt, so I always put the pressure on myself that I was supposed to be just like him.

Even though it was one of the hardest things I had ever done, on the first day of wrestling practice I went up to my dad and told him I wanted to do indoor track because track was always one of my favorite sports, and walked home. As I walked into my driveway, my mom pulled in behind me. Before I knew it, I was crying into her arms, telling her dad was never going to love me again. My mother drove me back to school, and I ended up in the wrestling room finishing up the first day of practice with my teammates.

My first junior varsity wrestling season was awful, and I still don't know how I ended up back in the wrestling room that day I walked home. If there wasn't enough pressure from being the legend's son, I also had to wear a singlet. Singlets are basically tights that wrestlers wear, and with my 215-pound physique it was no pretty picture for the girls I had crushes on. Also, there was the chance I could lose.

I would do anything to get out of wrestling. Whether it was practice where I would stay as long as physically possible in Mrs. Dauphin's room saying I was getting help, or matches where I physically made myself sick so I couldn't wrestle, I would do anything if it meant I didn't need to go out on that mat.

One night, things got so bad that my mother walked into the men's locker room while everyone was out in the gym and told me to grow up while I made myself sick in a toilet. Although she should have been in the bleachers waiting to go out with my dad because it was senior night for my brother, she was right there in the locker room with me basically telling me I was being a child. That wasn't even the most embarrassing moment of my season because our team would go on without me to win that match where I was hunched over a toilet, but later on in the season I wouldn't be as fortunate.

It was the last tournament of the year, and after a long season including being sick from sinus infections, stomach bugs, and anxiety I was ready for it to be over. That day I had a little bruise on one of my arms, and I used it as an excuse to not wrestle in the tournament. I felt no remorse until it hit me when we were weighing in and I had to tell my coach again in front of everybody that I wasn't wrestling. None of my team members seemed to care and on went the tournament. But it was obvious from my perspective that there was a lack of team leadership, our team wasn't wrestling at their best, and all I was doing was sitting in the stands. The worst was when a volunteer coach who was working with me all season showed up, and when I told him I wasn't wrestling I could see the disappointment written all over his face. That day I let my team down.   I honestly wanted nothing to do with wrestling ever again at this point, but something changed for me. I decided on a last minute whim to travel with my dad to the New York State wrestling tournament with varsity members of the team, and on this trip I began to see wrestling in a whole new light.

It wasn't that I had never seen wrestling as a community, because that was one of the aspects I liked about it the most, but at this tournament I started to really understand what that meant. I had a great time, became closer with my fellow team members and wrestling community, and by the end of the tournament I was ready to train and go kick some butt. But track season was starting, and that would keep me busy in the meantime.

Track was my favorite sport, but that was probably because, like academics, it came naturally for me. In junior high I set the record for throwing the discus as well as placing 1st in every meet except one. Also, the best part of it all was track was mine— my dad had no place in it. At the beginning of the season I was throwing between 90 and 100 feet, which was good for an incoming freshman. The only rude awakening was that all track members, even the throwers, had to participate in running. Although it was still pretty easy for me, I would struggle with my breathing even when I wasn't running, and I was diagnosed with a really bad sinus infection right off the bat.

One weekend in the middle of March I was at my cousin's birthday party, and I literally lay on the couch complaining of how I couldn't breathe. At this point I wanted to be home playing video games and relaxing, but my mom said if I was that bad then we needed to go to urgent care. That began a spiral downwards. When they tried to take blood, I went down hard. I woke up to a horrible smell, which I believe was smelling salts to keep me from passing out, but I was ready to knock that doctor out because of the stench. By the end of the night we were sent home, I was given steroids instead of the regular antibiotic regime to treat another bad sinus infection, and my mother was dumfounded with my diagnosis.

After my horrific experience at urgent care with my mother, we kept looking for what could be the source of all my sinus problems because I still wasn't getting any better. At a routine dentist visit we learned that my wisdom teeth were at a point where they were ready to come out, so we figured that they were the culprits. We hoped that getting them removed would solve everything, so we met with someone who could perform the surgery. After many trips up to discuss and go through surgery prep, I finally got them removed, but when I woke up from the anesthesia there were more problems than the regular pain and discomfort. I had gotten Bell's palsy, and the whole left side of my face had drooped. It was so bad that my eye actually had to be taped shut at night, but my doctors said it was just a temporary side effect from the anesthesia. The pain for having my teeth removed was tough to bear, but the Friday after my surgery I lost it. I had an intense anxiety attack, and I kept telling my mom that I was suffocating. After getting me back to bed I slept through the night, but the next morning she insisted we go to the doctors, who I felt like we were seeing every other day. That morning I just wanted to sleep and like any Saturday morning, play video games, but my mother could not bear going through another night like that, so off to the doctors we went.

That morning was April 3, 2010, and my regular doctor wasn't even in the office. We ended up seeing the other doctor at the practice, which was just icing on the cake that morning. He looked me over, went out of the room with my mom, and when they came back in my mom told me that we were going to the hospital.

I was furious because it was a Saturday morning, when cartoons and video games should have been a priority, but I was too weak to put up a fight. After getting my father from our house we headed right up to the hospital. Doctors were already waiting for us when we arrived. The next thing I remember was sitting in a room on one of those strange gurney-beds at the Upstate Golisano Children's Hospital in Syracuse New York, and I asked my dad for a cup of water because I was thirsty. Right after drinking it I yelled at my dad to get me a bucket, and I threw it all back up. My dad began to rub my back, but then my mom came back in the room to grab him. Before I knew it they were both gone.

I found myself alone, stuck watching television in the room. I just wanted to go home. Thoughts ran through my head. What was taking my parents so long?

The next thing I remember is my father coming back into the room with a look of fear on his face I could never have even pictured before that moment. The words that were about to leave his mouth couldn't even match the fear I saw on his face. "Tim… things aren't good. You have cancer. Please don't worry. You have over a 70% chance of beating this." Those words changed my life immediately, but the day wasn't over yet. It was about noon when I entered the hospital that day, around 2 pm when my dad delivered the news, and by 4 pm I was on my way to receive my first bout of chemotherapy. Everything happened so fast. The doctors knew I was very sick and every minute was precious. I wasn't told at the time, but I had a tumor the size of a football inside of my chest, and if I hadn't gotten treated right away, it would have suffocated me. I can remember having procedures done that day, but other than that, the only thing I remember was the desire to be surrounded by my family and close friends. Even more, I wanted to call certain people, like my best friend Hannah, but my mom thought it would be better for her to contact Hannah's mom, and other close family and friends in my life to let them know what was going on.

Hannah was like a sister to me. After meeting in second grade when our mothers worked together, we formed an instant friendship. Although this sometimes turned into a sibling rivalry because we both played soccer as kids and did well in school, there was no one I would rather spend time with. Even when we wouldn't spend as much time together because our class schedules, sports schedules, and everything else was pulling us in different directions, when we did find the time to hang out or catch up it was like we had just seen each other the day before. I trusted her, and she trusted me, so that is why when I heard I had cancer I felt I needed to let her know.

10

And as weird as it sounds I was almost relieved with my diagnosis. I knew something was wrong with me and this validated my complaining, but for once in my life I wouldn't be glad to be right. Somehow, I knew the C-word was going to come out of my dad's mouth before he even said it.

While everything happened rapidly, there were flashes and moments I will never forget. I will never forget the look on my grandma's face when she saw me in the hospital bed for the first time— she had lost her first child and only daughter at 2 years old to the same disease. I will never forget the sound in my mom's voice when she talked on the phone to tell my other family members and close friends what was going on. And I will never forget the disbelief going through my head. Was this really happening to me?

After my initial treatment, a lot of tears, and a lot of visitors from my community, things were starting to become normal again, or, at least, as normal as things could be. Plus, I was taking biology at the time, so during procedures I was able to ask what was going on because I had just learned about some of these body processes in school. One scenario I remember specifically was getting a scan of my heart done, and I was talking about the different parts of my heart that were on the screen with my doctor. Fortunately he was just as interested in discussing everything with me. I remember my mother joking that only I would be talking about stuff I learned in class with the cardiologist. But for me it was just trying to take my mind off the C-word.

One of the big moments after my diagnosis was when I got to eat solid food again, which I hadn't done since my wisdom teeth surgery. I remember exactly what I had— a double quarter pounder with just cheese from McDonalds. Not the most health-conscious meal, but it was the only thing I wanted at the time. It was tough to eat, but I enjoyed every second of it.

After returning home from a five-day stay in the hospital, I had to start getting acquainted with what would be known as the "new normal." This meant going back to school while still receiving my weekly chemo treatments. Much to my dismay, participating in track was out of the question.

I didn't like being back at school, and there were a lot of things that were different. A lot of it was me, but hearing that I had cancer also impacted a lot of my peers and community members. I still had my Bell's palsy, which made me feel very self-conscious, especially in front of the girls in my grade because the left side of my face was drooping downwards. Some days I had to be attached to an IV for fluids or chemo treatments, so I would walk around with that stuck in my arm. Plus, wherever I went it seemed like I always had someone watching or monitoring me. Everyone was overly concerned about me in ways I wished they weren't. Or they wouldn't interact with me at all.

Eventually, I could no longer go to school in person because it was too physically and emotionally taxing. Instead, I went to school through a distance learning system. Basically, I would Skype into my classes, but instead of going through a computer there was one polycom device in my house, and one on a cart being pushed around to my classes at the high school. Even though this was still weird, I felt like my distance learning system gave me more control over how I presented myself to my peers, and on days where I didn't feel up to it I could turn the screen off so nobody could see me. To my satisfaction, this meant I could go to class in my pajamas some days.

Thankfully I had amazing tutors, teachers, and a mother who was involved with administration for education so she knew everything that I was legally entitled to. I finished out the year completing all of my state exams and got marks all in the high nineties. Things seemed to be looking up in my life.

By June, my peers and I had come to grips with the fact that I had cancer, or at least as much as a bunch of young teenagers could. Many people were telling me online that they loved me and hoped I'd get better soon, through a website called Caring Bridge. Community members stopped by my house all the time to see my family and me, along with bringing food and goodies. I was well fed to say the least. Pretty much the new normal had set in, and I didn't think it was a bad life at all.

Chapter 2 Sightless in a Sighted World

On Saturday July 17th of 2010, in the middle of the summer, I woke up and noticed my vision was a little fuzzy. I waved my hand back and forth in front of my face while I was lying in bed staring at the window, and noticed the worst of the blurriness was a shadow in the shape of a crescent moon in the leftmost part of my left eye. I figured I had been playing too many video games and watching too much TV, so I shrugged it off. Of course, that is what I wanted to believe in my heart, but I had learned that the luxury of shrugging small changes off was no longer something I had. I needed to let someone know about it. I called my mother from downstairs up to my room, and told her what was going on. Like me, she wanted to just dismiss it as something that wasn't worth getting worried over, but like me, she also knew that wasn't an option. The next thing I remember is begrudgingly riding in the car to the hospital, a drive I did too often. Once we had arrived at the emergency room, we waited to be seen. After waiting for what seemed like forever, I was finally seen by some doctors, including the on-call oncologist. The consensus was that everything was fine and I was good to return home. In reality though, it wasn't.

As my mom remembers it, soon after they were about to send me home, two young doctors fresh out of medical school started their shift. They were tasked with telling me what was going on, and when they came into the room, my mom could tell they had never given bad news before. Apparently, my loss of vision could either mean my cancer was back, I had a brain tumor, or I had had a stroke. From that moment, everything moved so fast. I don't even remember the shock of hearing my cancer could be back, or that I possibly could have a brain tumor. My mom was on the phone calling my dad, who was at a golf tournament, and telling him get to the hospital immediately. Doctors and nurses were coming in and out monitoring me and getting me ready to go up to the Children's Hospital. And the talk of what to do next was echoing everywhere.

As a cancer kid, you begin to learn certain tricks to the trade. For example, you never want to be in the hospital on the weekend, because it means the best doctors aren't there. This particular weekend, I had two run-ins with this. First, I needed to see a specialist about my eyes but no one would be in until Monday. Even worse, I needed a spinal tap but no anesthesiologists were working. On Sunday the 18th, I received my spinal tap but unlike any I had before, I would be awake and only using painkillers combined with local anesthesia, which explains why I can remember the immense pain so vividly. My dad had to hold me in a wrestling cradle because I didn't want to stay still, the doctor kept trying to put the needle in but couldn't get it to go in right, and I was screaming "Take it out!" like I had never screamed before. After three attempts, the doctor realized it wasn't going to work, and in complete shock, pain, and disbelief, I was wheeled back to my room, where out of complete exhaustion, I crashed and fell fast asleep.

Although Sunday was horrific, Monday wouldn't be much better, but fortunately, my oncologist was back in town and taking control of the situation. I still had a little bit of my vision left at this point, but it was getting worse and worse by the hour. The doctors determined that I had cancer cells that were building up in my optic nerves. Relapsing in the optic nerves happens to less than one percent of leukemia patients but, of course, it was happening to me. I needed to have surgery to lance my optic nerves and relieve the pressure, but the only specialist on the east coast was hiking in the Adirondacks. Through friends, the wrestling community, and the pediatrician who originally sent me to Golisano for my initial diagnosis, we were able to track down the doctor and get an operating room quickly reserved so that we could make what my parents called the "Hail Mary" attempt to try and save my vision. That day I ended up having a spinal tap, chemotherapy, the surgery to lance my optic nerves, and my first bout of radiation to my optic nerves to try and save my vision. Before I was wheeled away to my long list of procedures, I will always remember what happened next. I called my mother back into the room they were wheeling me into, grabbed her face in both of my hands, and let her know If I was going to lose my vision completely, I wanted her beautiful

15

face to be the last thing I may ever see. I ended up losing my vision by the end of that day, and that moment before surgery when I looked into my mother's eyes was for the last time.

When we arrived for my first bout of radiation they put me in the machine, and I wasn't sure what to expect. I pictured myself glowing neon green or something crazy like that because this was the same material in nuclear power plants that powered cities, and too much of it could kill someone. As they started the machine, my mother, father, and Uncle Pat were waiting outside the room. From the other room they heard a 'pop.' The people working my procedure then came out and informed my family that they couldn't perform radiation that day because the machine was broken. Thankfully it didn't break mid-procedure and fry me, although I doubt that can really happen. I wasn't in the same room when this happened, but needless to say when the people working told my mom, she was already exhausted, and this news just made her furious. When my dad and uncle saw her red face, they took a step back and told the doctors that she was going to blow. She called for the Head of Pediatric Radiation and read them the riot act. She wanted the machine fixed or to have me brought to another hospital that could do it. We all knew this was the last chance I had to get my vision back, and she wasn't just going to give up. My mother went straight to work calling in a few favors and arranged to have me transported to another hospital for the radiation. At the same time, an older hospital employee was walking by on his way to clock out. He overheard my mom talking to the doctor, and told her if she gave him a minute to call his wife then he would stay and fix the machine. He did just that. Within an hour I had my first bout of radiation. Mama bear made sure her cub had what he needed.

Once the initial damage from the relapse was done, and the initial crisis was averted, the next talk on the table was how I was going to survive now that my cancer was back. Blindness wasn't even a concern because this was life or death. My doctors ended up deciding on a bone marrow transplant for my best chance for survival, and as soon as they did, my family members got tested to see if one of them could be my donor. My parents and brother were tested, but my brother had the highest likelihood to be a match. As predicted, my parents were not

16

matches, but to our surprise my brother was not only a match, but absolutely perfect. We fought like crazy, but a sense of relief swept over my family when we learned he could be my donor, and I may have even wanted to hug him.

Finding a donor was the first step, but after that we had to choose where to receive my transplant. Based on proximity, the procedure I needed done, and the high standards my parents expected out of the hospital, we narrowed down the search to a few options. Ultimately, we decided on Boston Children's Hospital, and Boston would soon become home. But it wasn't quite that easy. Before we left, I faced daily fears and frustrations from losing my vision, and had to put up with the long five-hour trips back and forth to Massachusetts in order to have everything set for the transplant. On the bright side, the community put together a huge benefit before we left, and it was like nothing else. My entire community came together to support my family and I, and together they raised tens of thousands of dollars for us to help with expenses and costs that began to pile up very fast. I remember thinking at the time how I would never be able to thank my community and its members for everything they have done. But the next part of my cancer journey was right around the corner.

I officially arrived in Boston that year on August 24th. Our new home was the Ronald McDonald House down the street from Boston Children's Hospital. Although it wasn't my house in Fulton, I began to figure my way around by touch, and because it wasn't that big I had enough strength to walk around our room without the assistance of a wheelchair. One of my biggest memories of staying at the Ronald McDonald House was when I celebrated my 16th birthday party on the porch outside of the main building. It wasn't much, compared to our usual huge parties with bouncy houses and water slides every year, but some of my family members had driven up for the day, and together, we had some birthday cake on the front porch. At that point my family and I were celebrating every opportunity we got.

I was originally supposed to have my transplant on September 3, 2010, but it ended up being pushed back a week because I kept getting fevers. As a cancer kid at Boston Children's Hospital, I quickly learned true fevers only counted if they reached 101.4 °F, nothing like the 99° F that earned you a day home from school. Luckily, I ended up being able to receive my transplant only a week later than originally planned thanks to a break in the fever, but that didn't eliminate the fear and panic everyone in my life was experiencing, thinking the procedure was never going to happen. Or the scarier scenario my parents would whisper of not soon enough. My fevers finally subsided, and the week before I was going to receive the transplant I entered the hospital to receive doses of chemo and TBI (total body radiation) to make sure there were no traces of cancer left in my system before my procedure.

Soon after receiving the transplant things went downhill. I don't remember much, but I know I ended up in the ICU (Intensive Care Unit) right away, and would soon be on a regiment of a morphine pump that went off every 15 minutes, and medical marijuana. Also, my heart, lungs, and kidneys were failing, and things kept getting worse. Not to mention that once you have a bone marrow transplant, your immune system resets, so I was in isolation because the slightest illness could kill me, and I was too weak to eat or really even sit up in my bed. After things kept progressively getting worse, my doctors told my parents to start preparing for what was about to come, my parents started contacting family members to say their last goodbyes.

Thinking back now, that was it for me. My doctors didn't believe and my parents were forced to acknowledge that everything they had done might be for nothing. I can just picture myself lying there in bed with all sorts of lines coming out of my body, getting nutrients in place from a bag, receiving dialysis, oxygen, and who knows what else to keep me alive just a little longer. The weirdest part of it all is I don't remember any of it. The most I can remember are different dreams or uncomfortable feelings, but that is it. My mom says I'm lucky. I'm sure there are moments she wishes she could erase.

Even though I had been basically written off, I am blessed enough to be here today. What really happened I don't think we will ever know, but through the combined efforts of my team of doctors, the prayers I had pouring in from all over the country, and my own stubbornness—at least according to my mom—my body eventually stabilized. Then I began the long, long road to recovery. After 46 days, my body finally began to engraft – my brother's cells were now doing all of the work within my body.

Eventually I became strong enough to leave the intensive care unit, but I was still under many restrictions because my immune system was so weak. I was still receiving my nutrients through an IV and I was so physically beaten down that I was unable to really get up or walk. One of the concerns that needed to be addressed right away was how I would get physical therapy, because every day I spent bedridden meant I would become even weaker and weaker. Sadly, as great as Boston Children's Hospital is, it did not have a physical therapy center for its children going through transplants. Because of this problem, as soon as I was deemed strong enough, I was moved back to Upstate Golisano Children's Hospital where they could offer me the services in a sterile environment. Although it was exciting to return to my state, my body still wasn't strong enough to go back to my house, and in order to get back to Syracuse, I had to endure one of the longest rides of my life—in an ambulance. I needed to be strapped to a stretcher in the ambulance the entire ride, and even when I asked if I could get resituated or roll to my side because I was severely uncomfortable, the response was a big "no". Needless to say I was not too happy when I arrived at Golisano, but I know my parents were very happy to be back in our home territory.

Once arriving back to Golisano, I could start receiving physical therapy. But at this point, the muscles in the fronts of my legs had atrophied, and I was unable to lift my feet when I was up. Not only that, but even with two people holding me up by a Gait belt and holding onto a walker, I could barely stand. I remember days when the goal was literally just to sit in an actual chair out of my bed for an hour or get thirty steps before having to sit back down in my wheelchair, which was always close by. Although it sounds like strength problems were the only thing holding me back, my blood counts of platelets, hemoglobin, and who knows what else were still struggling to reach levels that they needed to reach, and every day brought on its new troubles. I had just started to eat food again, but very sparingly, so I still received my nutrients through an IV. I had to deal with the psychological and mental pressures of spending my year in isolation while continuing with school. Most of all, I had to come to grips with the fact that I was blind and nothing in the near future was going to change that.

After 100 days spent in the hospital, I finally was able to return home. Even though it was great news, especially because my goal was to return home before Christmas, I remember being angry because no one wanted to get my hopes up about possibly going home. They didn't tell me until the minutes before we left the hospital, fearing I couldn't handle any more disappointments in my life if it didn't pan out. But since I was blind, my mother packed up the entire room to go home without me knowing. I said some choice words at the time, feeling like everyone had taken advantage of my blindness, but overall I had a feeling of relief.

The good news came with its frustrations. I would need to confront some of my biggest challenges at the time. One was learning how to get in and out of my mother's Nissan Quest in my body's condition, blind. Two was being strong enough to get up the three steps into my house. Such small tasks were suddenly mountains to me. I had practiced the days before I would return home with my walker in the hospital. Finally, I had to come to terms that while I was returning home, I would be doing so without my sight.

In the end, being home was nice even with its problems. I was so weak that for the longest time I didn't climb the stairs to get into my bedroom, which meant the couch was my new bed. My mom didn't want to leave me alone, which meant a blown up air mattress was her new bed. I couldn't even make it to the bathroom to use the toilet because getting up from the couch required so much energy, so I used a commode. I was still hooked up to an IV for a majority of the day to receive nutrients because I wasn't eating, and I logged into school with a distance learning system even though I didn't do much, especially with having to leave my house so many times a week to get checked out by my doctors at Golisano, and once a month to Boston as well.

After a couple of months, I finally got to the point where tutors were allowed into my house including my TVI (teacher of the visually impaired). Even more importantly, my physical and occupational therapists were able to work with me. Gradually, I was able to integrate back into doing my school work and get caught up from what I missed. I relearned fine motor skills, such as how to tie my own shoes and button clothes. And after many hours of physical therapy, I was finally strong enough to switch from using my walker to using leg braces. Even though my mother was concerned with my schooling, we both knew the priority was to get my strength back. Strength meant getting back up the stairs, and getting back into our real beds. Although I was self-conscious about the leg braces, I made a lot of jokes like I was Forrest Gump. Even then, I was realizing it was better to look on the bright side then wallow in self-pity.

My year in isolation felt like forever at the time, but the next thing I knew it was over and we could begin discussing my return to the world. Looking back now, that year was hugely important in preparing me for the future. My life was certainly never going to be what I had thought it would, but I began to realize it didn't mean it had to be worse. While being able to see my friends was my motivation to get back to school, I still had to attend my classes, including AP World History, which I refused to drop. I ended up getting 4 out of 5 on that exam—it was one of my proudest moments. And just because I was in isolation and people weren't allowed into my house didn't mean there weren't loopholes, like porch parties. This is what we called it when my close family and friends would come over and stand outside, whether there was snow, rain, or extreme heat, and I would get to talk with them. When the cold winter of central New York was over with, I was able to sit down in a chair on the porch and talk to others as well. One of the biggest of these porch parties was at the end of the school year when my advisory class took a field trip to my house and we had a barbeque. It was amazing and so great at the time to see my friends, who had been with me throughout my whole journey, and who I had kept in touch with using the distance learning system. Also, they raised money through a can drive to get me a hammock outdoors which was great because it was another way for me to get around the restraints of isolation. Earlier in the winter that same advisory class had come and sang carols outside my house. The fact that we were all together again now, over just a few months, reminded me that things were going to get better even if that meant being sightless in a sighted world.

Chapter 3 What's in Me Is Stronger than What's in My Way

Returning to school my junior year was a difficult transition. I had to learn different techniques and systems so I could do more of my work without assistance, and had to learn how to navigate around with a cane independently to travel to my classes. On top of these issues, I was dealing with the fact that I was still always a sneeze or cough away from getting sick. The original plan when I returned was to only go a few days of the week and use my distance learning system from my home the rest of the days. Although I was furious about this, I knew it was realistically what I needed to do. After the first day of my 3-day week, I was devastated. I felt weird wearing my leg braces in public, I felt weird being surrounded by an entourage of people, I felt weird because my school had been remodeled since I lost my vision, so I really didn't understand the new layout of it. But probably the worst moment was when I almost passed out from exhaustion practicing walking to my classes, and someone had to run and get me a chair. It felt like everything I did, someone had to be right behind me, helping me along.

Even though it was a rough day and by the time it was over because I felt completely drained, I somehow was ready to try again and go back the next day. It was awkward seeing all of my friends, especially people who hadn't seen me in over a year, or the ones who didn't know how to interact with me now after everything had happened. Honestly, by the end of the week, I didn't want to go back. Thankfully I had a support network, including the most amazing mother in the world, and with her strength, I wasn't going to let anything stop me.

I want you to know that going back didn't mean I was out of the woods yet. I still felt depressed, I still felt isolated and different from everyone around me, and my mother still had to help pick me up at the end of some days. But aside from these feelings, something inside of me wasn't going to let me fail. I not only made it through my first week, but I never took a day off.

Even more important to me, I never had another moment where I had to sit down in the hallway because I was too weak to make it from class to class.

For the most part, school was great, and it was great being around other kids again. Also, even though I couldn't participate directly on the sports teams I was on before, I was still able to be a member of the football, wrestling, and track teams and go to as many events as I could. I put everything I had into school and the many hours spent at outpatient therapy every chance I got. In the end, it felt like it all led up to the moment I was free of my leg braces.

One day I just decided I wanted to stop wearing them. Of course there was more to the story, but that's how it started. After originally being diagnosed with cancer, I had the opportunity to receive a wish from the Make-A-Wish Foundation. I deliberated over it for a long time, worried I would mess it up as a 15-year-old. I thought of meeting celebrities like Taylor Swift, who I thought was cute and would make my friends jealous. Or maybe cooking lunch with the White House chef because I loved to cook, and then having lunch with the President. But it turned out a handshake with him was the best I could do. And of course there were the different schemes to get onto game shows to win money. Some of these wishes were flops, impossible, and at the time I wasn't confident enough to go through with any of them. And the next thing I knew I lost my sight and that changed everything. What was the point of some of these wishes if I couldn't even enjoy them?

Once I had gotten healthier and returned to school, I was contacted again by Make-A-Wish, and we began thinking about what I wanted my wish to be. I needed to get my wish in before I was 18 and I had turned 17 that August. Although it was great getting to think about it again, I honestly got a little depressed. I didn't know what I could do now that I was blind. I no longer had the drive to want to cook or meet chefs like I did in the past, and the only logical thing for me to do was something I felt comfortable doing blind. At first that meant Disney World, a place that I had been times before, where I could also swim with

24

dolphins at Sea World, and go to Universal. Although this sounded fun, my heart wasn't really in it and I wanted my wish to be unique. Thankfully, I hadn't decided anything yet, and that year I was given an audio book that changed my life. The book was *Touch the Top of the World: A Blind Man's Journey to Climb Farther than the Eye Can See*. It was about the life of the blind adventurer, Erik Weihenmayer. He had climbed the seven summits, including Everest. After listening to it there was no doubt in my mind what my wish was going to be, because I knew in my heart I needed to meet him. Not only did I want to meet him, but I wanted to adventure with him as well. After some planning from the Make-A-Wish Foundation and seeing whether Erik would be willing to grant my wish, I had my official Wish party at one of my favorite restaurants in Syracuse, New York, Tully's, and was told that I was going to get to meet Erik and we would go on an adventure together.

Once it was set that I was going to meet Erik, we began to plan what we would do. First, I had a conference call with Erik. Not only was I off-the-charts excited, but the call also went greater than I could have ever expected. I had a giant smile on my face the entire time, and laughed from joy when he asked if I wanted to climb a frozen waterfall with him. He specifically told my mother she shouldn't worry. By the end of the call I was more determined than ever to be physically prepared for whatever we were going to do. So motivated that later that night I told my mom I could no longer wear my leg braces. Although she was worried, she relented. I stood true to my word and never wore them again.

That summer of 2012 I met Erik, and it was better than I could have ever imagined. We went zip lining, where he enjoyed scaring me to death when we crossed a rope bridge that had missing planks and no handles over the Colorado River. I went from almost crying the first time I went whitewater rafting to jumping out of the boat and swimming in the Colorado River the third time through. I also went tandem biking, hiking, played air hockey, jumped on his trampoline, and even got to climb on the rock wall treadmill device he had at his house. We may have even driven Erik's ATV, but I'm not a witness. My wish was truly spectacular and something I will never forget, but what I did on that trip wasn't what made it so amazing; it was what came after. I had not only gained the confidence that I could do anything even though I was blind, but I had made a friend for life, which was honestly the best thing I could have wished for.

And if that wasn't a good enough summer, I also got to attend a 3-week program at the Perkins School for the Blind in Watertown, Massachusetts. This program would be the first time where I was able to interact with other blind teens, or in my case, blind people in general. I learned a lot when it came to mobility, braille, and skills I would need in my life to live on my own. But being around other blind teens I started I realized how much farther behind them I was, which was frustrating. Ever since my cancer I had people doing almost everything for me because of my physical weakness and inability to learn independence skills, so Perkins was my first opportunity where I would not only do things on my own since my diagnosis, but I had no choice. Just as I had learned through my junior year of high school, I had to work hard in order to succeed. I would no longer go through life with everything coming easy for me.

During those three weeks I went horseback riding, stand up paddle boarding, and even to petting zoo where I got to feel a hedgehog, giant snake, and other animals. Experiences so trivial before were exhilarating for me now.

But the main reason I was there was to learn how to navigate better with a cane, read more in braille, and work on basic things such as preparing food in a kitchen, taking care of dishes, and doing my own laundry – all things my mom was glad to hear. Although it may not seem like much, it was leaps and bounds beyond anything I had been doing. I began to feel a sense of pride I had never experienced before in my work, even if I had to begrudgingly accept that I was farther behind then my peers, many of whom were younger than me, like my roommate Nick.

I couldn't have asked for a better roommate, and I felt like Nick was an 11-year-old version of me in a lot of ways. He was smart, driven to succeed, and really good at a lot

26

of things including singing. We had a lot of fun together that week that included sacrificing our pride to get our nails painted so we could go up on the girl's floor. Maybe not the best idea, but it generated a lot of laughs, and by the end of the program we had formed a pretty tight bond after only three weeks.

Going back into my senior year I felt invigorated and filled with a drive to succeed. To start off the year, I was going to actually play football. At least to the extent my doctors would allow, because as they told me, "We didn't save your life for you to go out and throw it away." The deal was that they would approve my physical, but no contact allowed. Although I wasn't overjoyed, I took what I could and was happy for the opportunity. We tried to outsmart the system by having me snap for extra points, since players can't hit the snapper in that situation. But it never got to the point to where I could get into a game. The worst nights were homecoming and senior night. All of the seniors were supposed to get in, and what turned into a very close game amongst rival teams ended up with a lost opportunity for me. On the bright side, I was voted Homecoming King. But didn't make up for the fact that we lost, and my teammates felt that it was there fault I didn't get in the game, that if they would have just played harder than I could have. The night was tough, and I questioned why I stayed involved with football, but I kept moving forward and to my surprise I ended up making it into the last game of the regular season. We were down a lot in that game and with two minutes left on the clock, the coaches were calling my name to get me ready to go in and play center like I had before I got sick. The other coach agreed to not have the other team hit me, and we ended up going 61 yards in 3 plays. I completed three shotgun snaps I couldn't have even made when I was healthy.

Although we lost the game that night, you wouldn't have known it. Not only were both stands going wild when I got in the game, but when we shook hands the other team and coaches were congratulating me as if I was one of their own. The worst tackle I received that night was from a very emotional mother. It was like we won the Super Bowl, and on the bus ride home I was presented with the game ball. Even though we did not win our

27

first post-season game, something amazing happened. Although I didn't know about it, my coaches had submitted me as a nomination for a football award called the New York State Twelfth Man Award. I ended up being the recipient that year. The award normally goes to a player who sustains an injury and isn't necessarily able to play but still is able to motivate their team, but after reading about me the board decided I was the perfect fit. The night I received the award, one of the presenters told me he didn't know anyone so deserving win the award before. All that work I had put in was worth it.

As soon as football season was over, wrestling started back up. Not only was I excited to return to the sport I had almost given up on, my doctors also gave me permission to participate with contact. But even though I was a full participant, wrestling remained difficult for me. Not because I was blind, but because I was so weak. I ended up with the flu, sinus infections, and the stomach bug once or twice. I would throw up doing sprints at the end of every practice. I also learned that a side effect of my treatments was adrenal failure, which means my body would basically shut down if pushed beyond its limits from extreme chills and nausea, After getting this diagnosed, I was provided with medicine to treat it the best I could. But by that point, my body had already been through a lot and I ended up losing the strength that I had worked so hard to build up. The only varsity match I won that year was by forfeit, but even though it wasn't much of a consolation I knew I should celebrate the fact that any type of win was possible. Even better, I won a real match at the junior varsity level at a tournament. The name of the tournament was, ironically, The Blindsmens. But I was no longer judging my success by wins and losses – there was no point to that anymore. Instead, I considered how hard I worked, and how much I inspired my team. In that sense, it was my best season yet. Not only that, but at our end-of-the-year banquet, I was presented with a leadership award as well as the Ken Julian Award, which goes to a member on the team who isn't winning all of the matches, but every time they go out they give it all they have. It defined everything I was trying to be and do.

The last sport I participated in my senior year was track and field. Although I had already been involved the year after my isolation, it was honestly never the same for me after everything I had gone through. As a freshman in high school I thought track and field was my favorite sport, and it was also the one I thought I was the best at. I always imagined I would break the high school record, but that would never be the case. But I learned something most athletes never do. Sports aren't about recognition or having your name etched onto a trophy; they are about getting out, making a commitment to do your best and doing it, and most importantly enjoying what you are doing. A lesson everyone could use, athlete or not.

Beyond sports, I also participated in the National Honors Society, Class Officers, and math club. But all of that paled in comparison to attending Space Academy in Huntsville, Alabama. For one week, students from all over the world who were blind and visually-impaired could attend this program, and I was going to be a part of it.

I was also going to get to see my Perkins roommate Nick again. He had persuaded me to go with him to the program while we were in Boston. We were all supposed to meet at Perkins the day before flying down to Alabama, but I was shocked to find that Nick wasn't there. His brain tumor had come back, the same one that caused his blindness when it crushed his optic nerves during surgery. I sat with my mom that night and cried.

Although it wasn't easy, I knew I had to go for the both of us. The program had unique pins you could collect along the way from the different students attending from all over the world, and I was going to collect the best ones for him. Also, a woman told us about an award that only one camper received out of the hundreds who came from all over the world. I was determined to receive it, for Nick and me.

It was my first blind flying experience without my parents, and it was terrifying. Escalators, trams, and all sorts of obstacles at our layover in Atlanta threatened me each step of the way, but finally we arrived in Alabama. We were divided into groups. At first I had no one from the Perkins program in mine, but they switched me so I could have a few familiar voices around.

My mobility and braille skills at this point were still pretty bad, but I pushed myself whenever I could to try everything on my own. Although I felt like I hindered my team because of my limitations, I ended up being a key contributor. My brain was still functioning strongly, and in multiple activities I was able to emerge as a leader, assisting the members in my group to accomplish group challenges. One day we did a pool activity where our group had twenty minutes to swim to the other side of a pool while collecting different pieces of something that we would eventually put together. I still had the ability to visualize how things looked by touch, so once we had collected all the pieces I ran my hands over them to figure out what it was. I realized we had parts of a cube and set about giving my teammates tasks. I also made sure to include members on my team who were younger and weren't able to help with swimming, and by giving everyone a task we finished with many minutes to spare unlike the other group who ran out of time.

In addition to the learning and team challenges, we also got to go on different simulators like one that feels like walking on the moon, and another that feels like floating with no gravity. Also, by the end of the week I had collected a lot of pins for Nick, and I knew he would be impressed. As the program came to an end, our last major activity was the Quiz Bowl. My team wasn't winning by the final round so we wagered all of our points on getting the last correct answer. I came up with the winning answer for my team. On this high note, we prepared for the awards ceremony.

Although I had an amazing week, and learned a lot about space, leadership, teamwork and myself, the last piece was whether or not I won the award I set out for when I left Massachusetts. As the award ceremony commenced more and more people won awards, even a young girl from our group at

Perkins, but my name wasn't one of them. It hurt, and before I had cancer I probably would have stayed angry about it. But now, I thought about what an amazing week it had been, and I was OK.

But then the people MCing the event announced that there would be another award, and the presenter would be the award-winning author of *October Sky*. At that point my interest piqued again, but I didn't want to disappoint myself. But the next thing I knew I heard my name—I was so shocked that my friends had to nudge me to move. After receiving the award and shaking Homer Hickam Junior's hand, I returned to my seat where my team greeted me with enthusiastic cheering and pats on the back. After sitting in awe for the remainder of the ceremony, I went outside to see my leader from Perkins, who I had told back in Massachusetts I was going to win that award. She gave me a big hug. Then in tears I called my mother using her cell phone to tell her what I had just accomplished. Every achievement had been wonderful, but this one was the best yet.

By the time I graduated in June of 2013, on time, I was 7th in my class of 287. I also had 21 college credits. Between academics, sports, and relationships with my classmates and teachers I had accomplished so much even with my setbacks. My peers supported me so much that there was a section dedicated to me in our yearbook. I was truly blessed to have done so much in the face of so many obstacles. My senior quote sums it up perfectly: "Cancer may have taken a lot of things away from me including my sight, but it will never take my vision."

After graduating high school, the next big step in my journey was attending Ithaca College. Although it was a tough decision, I knew at the time I hadn't yet adapted the set of skills I would need to live independently, so I delayed admission to Ithaca for one semester and attended the Carroll Center for the Blind in Newton, Massachusetts. I participated in a 14-week independent living program, which I followed up with a 2-week intensive technology program. But before diving into all of this, I had two more things to do on my list.

31

During the summer of 2013 after my graduation, I attended a 5-week program in New York for visually impaired students who were either going to or preparing to go to college. The program was called STRIVE, and my program took place on the campus of Le Moyne College in Syracuse. Although I was going to attend an intense program at the Carroll Center before entering college, the program couldn't offer me the chance to live in an actual dorm environment, eat at a dining hall, and take mock classes. I greatly enjoyed the program, and as a result, became a better advocate for myself by immersing myself in the activities I would take part in at Ithaca, and made some great friends. I had done a lot of work to prepare for college, and I already knew where I would be going unlike most of the other students who were still in high school, so I emerged as a leader in the program. I also got ahead of the work for my mock classes, so in my spare time I created a guide for students still touring colleges, as well as provided elaborate notes from the content we were studying. Unfortunately I had to leave a few days early from the program and couldn't attend graduation. Before I knew it I was off to my next activity.

The reason I wouldn't be present for graduation was because I was off to attend my first No Barriers Summit in Telluride, Colorado. No Barriers is an organization that Erik Weihenmayer, who I met on my Make-A-Wish, was a founding member of and in 2013 he invited my family to come out for it. The summit was amazing. Telluride was an amazing city with so much going on, including a gondola to get from our hotel down into the city, different historical nature sites to explore, and many amazing restaurants including my favorite, an ice cream store called Telluride Truffle. While attending the summit I was able to participate in amazing activities such as rock climbing, hiking, and jumping on a giant trampoline where I was strapped in so I could jump over ten feet in the air. My favorite moments were getting to spend time again with Erik and his family, being in a place where people with an accessibility issue were in the majority, meeting and networking with so many amazing people, and most of all, hearing the amazing guest speakers at the summit. Bob Woodruff was there, Kyle Maynard, and even an actor who to my surprise only had one leg, but was one of the main actors in the comedy film Beerfest, which I had seen many times before losing my sight. And of course there was Erik who again I had to thank for making another profound impact on my life.

. I truly left the summit with a sense of accomplishment and a No Barrier Mindset: what's in me is stronger than what's in my way.

Chapter 4 Never Could Have Imagined in My Wildest Dreams

After concluding my programs at the Carroll Center, I started my first semester at Ithaca College, and I was ready for anything.

Although I'd like to say things were smooth by this point in my life, I still ran into a lot of obstacles when I arrived at college. The one that sticks in my head the most was that I returned to Ithaca during one of its worst winters in a long time, and I still had to learn my routes to dining halls, classes, and other important buildings on campus. I had the number for public safety in case I got lost in the new and rough terrain, but I was very stubborn and refused to use it. This stubbornness came to a head on a day where the wind chill was below 20 degrees. After wandering around for 20 minutes in the cold I gave in, but I was not happy, and again felt helpless even though I had just completed all of this training.

I was nervous to say the least, but as the weather improved so did I, and before I knew it I was taking the campus by storm. I joined many clubs, most notably the debate team, Colleges against Cancer, and Guiding Eyes for the Blind. Also, as if I wasn't pushing myself out of my comfort zone enough, I decided I wanted to do something crazy, so I joined the break dance team. A tall, dorky, not very strong guy isn't that great at break dancing as I learned, but the team was very accepting, so I had a lot of fun. My first semester at Ithaca ended up being great, and once the semester came to a close I had a 4.0 GPA. During the summer I would take on the next big adventures in my life.

I embarked on a trek through the Grand Canyon with No Barriers. Many people, who usually believed in me so much, like Erik and my mother, questioned whether this was going to be too much for me. But I convinced them and myself otherwise and set out on the trip. I started by flying into Arizona where I met up with our trip leaders and other students, some visually impaired, some not, and then we drove out to Flagstaff. After a long day of making sure we only brought the essentials with us, leaving everything else at a place in Flagstaff, we made it to our campsite on the rim of the magnificent Grand Canyon. After four days of camping, practicing hiking, learning about sound pollution, and engaging in other activities, we drove to the spot where we would begin the river portion of our trip. Our group would white water raft seven days in the canyon, camp out on sandy beaches at night, and hike nine and a half miles on the Bright Angel Trail out of the canyon. That was the piece everyone involved had feared for me.

On the first night of the river portion of our trip I was already having a blast and was ready for more. We had just come down a huge rapid before getting to our campsite, and after unpacking all of our supplies as a team, I found myself sitting in the hot sand facing out towards the water. What happened in that moment I can't quite put into words, but if I had to it was like I could see again. The noise of the water from the rapid we had just ridden was crashing by, the sound of the wind was blowing up against the canyon walls, the bugs in the bushes were making their noises, and in all of this natural noise I no longer felt I was blind. It was in this moment that I learned having sight had nothing to do with what it actually meant to see.

But not everything would be so easy. While we were boating we had to jump into the water to use the bathroom. One of these trips I was in the water and hit my head on something when I tried to surface. Next thing I knew I realized I was under the boat! No matter how hard I tried I couldn't get out, and I didn't know how much longer I would last in my panic. Luckily it was only my head under the boat so my guide was able to drag me out from the back of my life jacket, but he wouldn't let me get back into the boat. As he was pulling me back in he dropped me back in the water, saying I should try and get back in on my own. I was scared and not pleased about this, but after pulling myself up and getting dragged back in the raft by my fellow rafters, I got to calm down from my anxious state. Learning to be more self-sufficient was going to be a daily task.

I ended up having another troublesome moment, but for lack of a better word, it wasn't as exciting for me as surfacing under the boat. After a couple days on the river everything started to get to me, especially the sun. I hadn't been wearing enough protective clothing throughout the day, and my body had gotten too much sun. With pale skin I was already susceptible to skin cancer. And my adrenal failure kicked in.

I felt nauseous, all out of sorts, and all I wanted to do was get warm, comfortable, and sleep. Luckily we had gotten to camp that night before I was feeling at my worst, so I was able to find a spot in the sand to take medicine for stress and fall asleep. I wasn't too happy, and this moment reminded me of how weak my body still was, but my fellow rafters on the trek welcomed me back into the group just as if I were one of them after I felt better, and it made a huge difference for me.

The rafting portion of our trek soon came to an end, and the night before we set out on the daunting nine and a half mile hike, the team presented awards. I was humbled to receive the No Barriers Mindset award for never giving up in the face of adversity, but I felt the true magnitude of what that award meant the next day.

The next thing I knew it was morning. Together we all packed up camp, got our gear together for hiking, and got in the rafts one last time to cross the river to get to where the trail began. We started early in the day to try and beat the heat, but before we knew it the temperature was already in the high nineties. In addition to falling a couple of times, going very slowly because of my poor balance and mobility on the rocks, and having to stop so I could catch my breath, I was feeling defeated. At this point I had stress dosed multiple times for my adrenal failure, and my guide kept pouring water on me to keep my body temperature down. My adrenal failure already made me moody, but pouring cold water on me without notice did not improve my mood.

Eventually we reached the halfway mark around midafternoon, and even though we knew it was the hottest point of the day, we were still shocked to find the thermometer read 120 degrees.

Although the beginning of the hike was no walk in the park, as we continued after the halfway point things got harder and harder. I was exhausted physically and mentally, and the trek had pushed me to my limits. I began contemplating how much it would cost my mom's insurance to get a helicopter down here to get me out the rest of the way. Despite these thoughts I kept going somehow, and we reached another rest stop.

I thought I had to go to the bathroom when I arrived, but after sitting down to relax the feeling subsided, and I just wanted to keep going and get the trek over with. Additionally, the water at this stop was hot, so even though I needed to drink, it was grueling to get the water down. I had to channel my mother telling me to drink the awful medicine I had when I was sick, and thankfully that worked.

We started off again soon after our arrival at that rest point, but things got crazy again. We were hiking during the beginning of monsoon season in the canyon, so all of a sudden a storm, like nothing I had ever experienced, started. The rain came down in buckets, the thunder boomed like it was on my shoulder, the wind was blowing strongly, and I was glad not to see in that moment because of the lightning, which my teammates said was terrifying.

Once it had subsided we continued on, but I was soaked. This began to bother me, so I took off my shirt and just wore my rain jacket. It chafed my skin, and on top of that I realized I didn't go to the bathroom at the last stop, which my stomach was making sure to remind me. Eventually after some more stress dosing that brought me to a limit I had never dosed at before, exhaustion, and who knows what, we got very close to the next rest stop. That was until another group member yelled out for us to stop.

There was a 5-foot rattlesnake spread out across the trail, and I was a couple feet from walking with my guide right on top of it. Thankfully we stopped in time, but the snake wouldn't move because of a squirrel teasing it. I needed to use the bathroom so badly; I asked if I could just stab the snake with my trekking pole so we could continue onward.

After the squirrel ran away the snake slithered off the path enough for us to scoot by safely. Before I knew it we were at the next rest stop. And my first stop was the restroom.

Once I had concluded my business my group leader made me eat and drink some more, and because the other two groups from our team had made it to the top already, one of the guides came back down with some more food and water because our supplies were low. At this point I was ready to be done, and with only one and a half miles left I could taste it. Before we left though the guide who came back down gave me a Snickers. Just like that I got a burst of energy. I went the fastest I had gone all day for the last mile and a half of the trail, and after about thirteen and a half hours of hiking I was at the top.

I had a feeling of accomplishment like I had never experienced before. Between all of the doubts, all of the training just running up and down the stairs in my house, and everything I had faced that day, I had done it. As Erik says, it was a day where I could recognize that I had entered as a boy, and had come out as a man.

Although this adventure was a game changer for me, I was setting off again for another monumental experience that summer. That experience was a program called LEAP, held on the UCLA campus. The LEAP program was all about helping educate and inspire some of the brightest minds from youth all over the world and providing them with the strategies and tools to accelerate them ahead in life in order to be successful. The acronym stands for Leadership Excellence Accelerating Potential. After hearing about it from another student my first semester at Ithaca, I knew I wanted to be a part of it, and I applied for a scholarship to attend. Thankfully, I was lucky enough to receive one.

Although I was very excited at first about this new experience, especially because it was the first time I had applied to do something that wasn't just for visually impaired students, quickly I wasn't impressed. The program didn't realize that I was blind and would need assistance in making the event accessible, which I found confusing because that was what I wrote my whole scholarship essay on. At one point they were going to pay for my flight and send me back home. I was in tears and called my mother on the other side of the country, where it was past 2 a.m. I was devastated to say the least, but some members of the program had my back, and I was able to stay and receive special accommodations for the week. Not only did I learn a lot about myself, but I also took away so much amazing information from listening to so many incredible speakers. I networked and became friends with people including mentors for the future, and I believed I was getting the experience all students were supposed to have.

Everything was going quite well, but after my rough beginning to the week I was still down in the dumps. That was until one day my friend and roommate for the program, Stuart, who had been assisting me around the campus was talking to me, and said something nobody had ever told me before. He said that I had gone through so much, and everything I had done in my life was amazing, but me being depressed and dwelling on everything I had accomplished wasn't going to get me anywhere in life.

At this point in my head I was angry, thinking to myself *didn't you hear what I have been through over the last few days*, but after a few moments I realized he was right. Not only was he right, but he was also the first person I had ever been around that told me the honest hard to hear truth. I thank him so much for that, and in that moment I realized that life wasn't what had happened to me, it was what I chose to do with what had happened to me.

Soon I was invigorated to continue full force with the program, and I walked up with him to the front of the auditorium like all of the other students did before each session and danced.

I was embarrassed out of my mind, but I had the choice to live in that moment, and I wasn't going to sit back and let life happen to me anymore. The week would only go on to get better from that point.

Besides my bad breakdance session, which everyone loved anyway, I got the chance to participate in a speech competition. Channeling everything that had happened to me over the week, the amazing lesson I learned, and my burning desire to share my story with the entire program of 400 students from all over the world, I gave speeches that got me all the way to the final round on the big stage.

When I got up to speak I was in my prime. It was what I had endured and worked so hard for, and I was not going to blow it. The next thing I knew the tournament was stopped. I was told people were standing on their chairs going nuts clapping, and the head of the program came up on stage telling me how amazing I was. I thanked my friend Stuart and my other close friend Avery who was an assistant coach in my group that helped me out a lot during the week. Needless to say I felt like I was on top of the world at that moment, and I started to cry, and then called my mother to tell her what I had just done.

I was the winner of a speech competition plaque that year, and with everything I had learned I was ready to take on the world and go back to college. Before I knew it though, another year had passed at Ithaca. I received all As again and I branched out to even more activities. Most memorably, I became a senator for the Student Government Association. I also attended Ithaca's cross-cultural leadership retreat, the BOLD conference, and an alternative spring break trip where I volunteered to work with underprivileged kids at a youth center in Salamanca, New York.

The Alternative Spring Break trip was life changing for me. Every day I, along with our faculty advisor and 5 other Ithaca College students, would get up and go work with underprivileged children who couldn't be more excited to know that we were there to spend time with them. Although a lot of kids weren't sure what to think of me at first, once I was out playing dodgeball with them they thought I was the coolest guy around. By the end of the week every time we played I had about 4 kids surrounding me protecting me from getting hit and telling me where to throw the balls they handed me. One time I was the only person left on my team, so I daringly tried to throw my ball in the basketball hoop across the gym, which would bring everyone from my team back in. We all were surprised when the ball actually landed in the hoop. That led to instant fame among the kids because I got a basket without seeing, and at the end of the week I was sad to go.

Everything was great going into the summer of 2015 after another year of school, but I still ran into my fair share of obstacles my sophomore year of college. It was always crazy getting books made accessible at the beginning of the semester for my classes, so each new semester has its hiccups. Also, even with all of my activities, I still struggled with finding friends to just hang out with. Counseling, which I had started and continued with in college, sometimes helped. But it didn't make these moments any less emotional or hard.

One of the great things about my sophomore year was getting connected with the wrestling team on campus. I quickly befriended two of the guys on the team, Nick and Carlos, and they became two of my closest friends on campus. Also, in the spring of my sophomore year I went to my first party with them. Although it may not seem like much, and I didn't really drink because I take a lot of medicine, it was a big deal. The fact that I got off campus, was with friends having a good time, and wasn't in my dorm room alone like any other weekend night, meant the world to me.

As I entered summer again my schedule was pretty booked. I was going back to LEAP for a second time, and going to another No Barriers Summit. One of the cool things about this summit was that another member from my community, Ryan, was going to come with his family, and I couldn't wait to share with him the No Barriers experience that completely changed my life.

Ryan was in a bike accident before entering junior high, which left him paralyzed from the waist down and, like me, he was feeling the struggles of change. Once I learned about Ryan I was determined to get him to the No Barriers Summit, and with the help of our amazing community that dream became a reality.

The 2015 Summit in Park City, Utah soon became something very special for me, and I still joke around about how on the first night Erik was introducing me to everybody like I was the person everyone was there to see. I don't know what it is about that guy, but when I am around him I end up in my most humbling moments. Although I had to leave for the LEAP program before hearing Erik speak at the conclusion of the Summit, I was blessed with another amazing opportunity, and was glad my new friend Ryan got to be a part of it with me.

At LEAP, what started out as one of the worst weeks of my life the year before, turned into one of the most amazing. Even though I couldn't get a scholarship to attend the LEAP program again, I ended up paying to come back in 2015 because I had such a great time, but more importantly I had learned so much to help me be even more successful in my life.

In 2015 the theme of the program was "unstoppable," which I thought was great because I had just finished attending my second No Barriers Summit that was all about overcoming barriers in life. Also, to my surprise, one of the speakers was Mick Ebeling, who had spoken at the No Barriers Summit and would also be speaking at LEAP. They were having some technical difficulties for his speech, so I yelled up to him to ask how the rest of the No Barriers Summit was. To my surprise he then had me come up on stage and speak about No Barriers as well as introduce him.

It was the second time I had heard his speech over a 3-day period, but his message was so amazing and powerful that I was entranced just as much as the first time I heard it. After having been filled with the No Barriers and Unstoppable mind set for about a week, I knew that I needed to decide what I was going to do next that would push me out of my comfort zone.

I thought back to the Grand Canyon, and how amazing that feeling was when I made it to the top. After watching a video about someone who had summited Mount Kilimanjaro, I turned to my friend Robert, who was guiding me around the UCLA campus that week, and said "I am going to do that." Although I thought I was out of my mind at first, I applied the principles I learned through No Barriers, LEAP, and my life experiences, and by the end of the week it was clear that I was going to hike Mount Kilimanjaro.

I left that week on another high, and was again ready to take on the world and college, but I had one more journey before I returned for my junior year. In August I was going to get my first guide dog.

I started my program at Guiding Eyes on August 2 that year, and by August 4 I was introduced to my new partner in life, Lang. I don't know what it was, but I imagined getting a guide dog would be like the Disney experience where everything would be perfect, and I would say go somewhere and my dog would magically go to that place. But I was sadly mistaken. Not only do these dogs require a lot of work and training, but it was also the first time in my life when another living thing was completely dependent on me. I mean before I ate he needed to eat, before I went to the bathroom in the morning he needed to go to the bathroom, and I needed to know what he was doing all of the time to make sure he was safe, healthy, and not getting into trouble. It almost felt like I had adopted a kid, not a dog.

My training continued to be tough, and I honestly didn't know what I had gotten myself into. I waivered on whether or not I should keep Lang, but then I spoke to one of the dog trainers about the experience and it assured me what to do. They reminded me that a dog would be a priority in my life, but also a partner to help me with everything I struggled to do. I had a big decision to make, but like most things in my life I was ready to stick this out for the long haul.

After putting more emphasis into my dog as a priority, and accepting what our new life together would be like, things became easier and easier, and I could see this actually working out.

Three weeks had passed at the Guiding Eyes program and I was finally going to return home with my guide dog. I imagine it was a shock for him because we drove four hours from the guide dog center to my house in Fulton, and then after sleeping in my room just one night we were off to Ithaca where we would move into my dorm room. While I was trying to figure out the layout of the dorm my dog was with me, Lang peed on the floor in my room, At first I got really upset, but I eventually laughed it out, telling him "You are like all the other freshman now."

My first semester with Lang brought on its own challenges as every semester does, especially because I was frustrated that I could travel on my own faster and more efficiently without him, but immediately I noticed differences with my dog being with me on campus. Not only did I feel safer, but also more people were taking the time to stop and talk with me, or at least compliment Lang. The learning curve was definitely large for me considering I had never had a dog or a pet other than a guinea pig. But as my first dog, and life partner, I loved him.

Soon the fall semester was over, and I returned home for the winter break. These five weeks at home were something new for Lang, and I don't think he knew what to do when he had a whole house to run around in, but he adapted very well, and he was a joy to have around the holidays.

Once the five weeks were up, I traveled to Houston, Texas for an event called Presentation Power with my mentor, and now speech coach, Jonathan Sprinkles. Flying with Lang for the first time I wasn't sure what to expect, but we managed to get through everything fine, and once I arrived in Texas I met up with my friend Robert from LEAP, who had been brainstorming with me the project of climbing Kilimanjaro. We decided on calling the trip MounTimPossible.

My original goal was to just climb Mount Kilimanjaro as a way to prove to myself I could go on and do more in my life without limitations, but now it has become so much bigger. MounTimPossible is no longer just climbing a mountain; it is about living life to the fullest, making a difference in the world, and redefining what people see as possible. I won't just be climbing in May of 2017, but I will be raising $500,000 for organizations that have personally benefited me in my life, and I want to help them do that for others who are facing similar circumstances to mine.

I entered the weekend at Presentation Power not knowing what to expect. I had met Jonathan about a year and a half before, and after listening to him speak at the LEAP program in California, I knew I wanted to be just like him. His program was better than I could have ever imagined. I learned so much about speaking, branding, business, working well with others, and so many other skills I didn't have the chance to learn, so I plan to go back to the conference as many times as possible. Also, I signed up to have Jonathan become my personal coach, which is an investment I believe will pay off more than anyone could ever imagine.

After returning home with Lang from Texas, things only got busier. I returned to college the morning after I flew back and classes started on Wednesday of that week. Luckily my room was the same from fall semester, so my mother was able to bring everything back to college and setup my room while I was gone. I didn't have more than a few nights back before flying out with my dog on the Thursday of that week to attend a performance festival with my professor and two other students at Georgia Southern University. My flight with Lang was a little crazy because we had two layovers to get to Savanah, but he was a trooper and did great.

The day after we arrived we drove over to the college and began meeting the people who were in charge of the festival, as well as other students. It was a great environment, and I thought the people in charge were awesome, and as soon as we arrived Friday morning we got right into things. Different

45

students, professors, and performers began presenting their pieces, and I didn't present until Saturday. The piece I had been working on was my hike out of the Grand Canyon, and although I hadn't had too much time to work on it, I knew that I could tell my story well. When it was finally my turn to present I ended up doing a great job. And we made everyone laugh because every time I made noises to signal tripping and falling on my hike, Lang would jump up in the audience and try to run up to me on stage. One of our other activities was practicing and performing a piece on the spot, and Lang actually was a part of that performance; to no one's surprise, Lang stole the show and all the people loved him. Before we returned back to Ithaca we had a little party at one of the professor's houses, and Lang was in heaven because they had dogs, so he got to run around, play with them, and may have gotten some dog treats too.

The flights home were as smooth as the flights out and the only consequence of my trip was it put me behind in Financial Accounting; a class I already knew was going to give me trouble. I had missed the introductory concepts, so I was bound to struggle.

Before I knew it, Lang and I had accomplished ten flights together over a one-week period. And thanks to a lot of struggling, talking on the phone with my mother, and attending many office hours with my professors, it seemed like I was back on my feet. Having a sense of balance in my life again was good, because I was about to set out on accomplishing one of my next goals.

For the American Cancer Society's Relay for Life, I wanted my Tug for Tim team to raise over $5,000. Relay for Life was an event I participated in as a child before I had cancer, and I had participated in the year I was diagnosed and still had my vision. I have attended at least one relay event every year since. I even attended during my year of isolation and walked the survivor lap in my leg braces with my father holding me up by a Gait belt, which is basically a tight strap I would put around my body with handles for people to hold on to support me.

After asking for all of the money I would get for Christmas to be donated, holding an event where I spoke about my journey with cancer, and painting myself purple to raise money, we were well over $4,000. When the date of the relay came we were close, and with the onsite fundraisers we had there was no way we wouldn't hit our goal.

All of a sudden it was 9 pm, and we were still $180 short, and my amazing team of loved ones who were running the onsite fundraisers needed to head back home. At that point I didn't know what to do, so I called my mom who offered to pay it so I would stop worrying, but then I started doing math in my head. I realized that if I sold 15 more Tug for Tim shirts, that were $12 apiece then we would have exactly $5,000. With some perseverance and help from my friend Johnny who had spent the entire day with me working and fundraising, we went around telling people at the event what we were trying to do. In about an hour we had broken the number of t-shirts we needed to sell to hit our goal. It was amazing to have actually done it, and I thought about all of the people like me who had or were still dealing with cancer that would benefit from the money. The American Cancer Society has done so much in the fight against cancer and because of everyone who was a part of the Tug for Tim team they now had $5,000 more to continue doing their amazing work.

Once the relay was over, I was approaching finals week, so I needed to focus on catching up in all of my classes because I had let school go by the wayside when I was fundraising. Sleep became a luxury, not a necessity. Between struggling to access books, writing so many essays in a short period of time, dealing with complex accounting problems, and who knows what else at that point, my stress levels peaked out. When this happens my mother still gets a call, and I let her know I had bitten off way more than I can chew, so I needed someone to vent to and some guidance. Although it took a lot of work, including many hours with my professors and teacher's assistants, I was able to steer things back on course again, and received the grades I strived for. In one of my classes, my professor actually liked my policy paper so much that she asked if she could use it in the future as a guide for what she wanted from students.

Everything was going really well as the semester came to a close, but even though I was hitting high grades on all of my assignments, there were just so many that I couldn't manage to get them all done. I almost ended up having to take an incomplete in one of my courses, but thankfully I was able to finish the 3,000 word essay just before papers needed to be submitted. I was finally able to return home and catch my breath, but I just wanted my grades more than anything. Eventually I got them, and I was very happy to know I received an A in all of my courses, bringing my GPA up to a 3.98.

Although finally getting home after a long semester and getting a second to relax was nice, as my mother says I don't let grass grow under my feet and off I went again. I started working out with a trainer at the gym up the street from my house, swimming in the local pool, and getting out to walk and hike as much as possible to continue to get in shape for my climb. I also started putting a lot of focus on the MounTimPossible project, which included investing even more time with my coach Jonathan Sprinkles. All together, things were good and I enjoyed what I was doing because I was so motivated, and the next thing I knew it was June when I would embark on my next adventure.

I traveled to Colorado to meet up with my partner for the climb, Robert, where we would hike together and attend the No Barriers Summit at Copper Mountain, Colorado. When Robert and I first connected after I landed at the airport in Denver, we got to catch up while driving to our hotel at Copper Mountain. The next day we would go on our first hike together, and although it wasn't easy at that altitude, it was very successful and we learned a lot about working together. On top of the physical activity, we worked on getting more information sorted out for our Kilimanjaro climb and making plans for raising the $500,000. Then we moved on to the No Barriers Summit.

Now when I originally went to the summit I was signed up for four different events to participate in, which ranged from a ninja obstacle course to dragon boat racing. Well, it turns out I didn't attend any of the things as I planned. The first day of events I participated in an adaptive skateboarding event. Although I was scared, the people running the event were great, and I actually managed to do some tricks on the board with assistance. At one point we went down a ramp where I was scared out of my mind, but the best part was when I made it down safely and asked how high the ramp was—hey said, "it was only two and a half feet." While they may have not thought it was a big achievement, in reality it was. I overcame my fears that day, and by doing so I got some great video, but more importantly had a great time doing something I never imagined I would ever do.

The other event I attended at the summit was hiking up Copper Mountain with Erik. Again I wasn't signed up for it, but Erik insisted I do it because it would get me one step closer to the top of Kilimanjaro, and how could I argue with that. Robert and I worked really well together again, but what started off easy got tougher at the end. We flew through the beginning of the trail, but towards the end there was a steep rocky area that really pushed me. I stopped a lot, kept asking "are we there yet," but eventually we made it through that section and made it up our last part of the trail to the top. That day, with Robert's help, I summited my first mountain! It was a huge success, and would be one of many on this trip.

The summit concluded on a Sunday, and before I would go back with Erik and his family to Golden, Colorado, we were going to stop and climb my second mountain. The terrain for this mountain was more difficult than what we experienced at Copper, but after some frustrating moments, by mid-day we had summited my second mountain, Mount Royal. Erik says the true summit isn't until you are back down safely, which I believe wholeheartedly now, and although it was rough coming back down, I learned so much about hiking on this trek and knew it would better equip me in the future because of it. But being a beginner at anything is rough, so everything tested my self-confidence.

Eventually we ended up at Erik's house then traveled out to his ranch. While we were there I learned how difficult it is to swim across a lake at 9,000 feet elevation, conquered my fear of swinging from a rope swing out into the lake, and attempted to solo stand up paddleboard. Although I was not excited for the paddle boarding, I was talked into it. It was not pretty. I started on my stomach and thought it was going great, but they wanted me to stand up. I eventually progressed to my knees, and fell into the cold water a lot. At one point, with people supporting me by letting me put my hands on their heads while they kneeled on their boards, I finally stood up, but then fell right back in. On my last try I got to the point where I wobbly stood up, grabbed the paddle quickly, and officially did one paddle while standing up. I know I have a lot of room to grow in the future, especially because my balance stinks, but I was ecstatic to even be up for one paddle and satisfied with my accomplishment. Even if I then fell back in the water again. Although I kept falling in the water, I found out I was like a pro at getting back on to my board. The day at the ranch definitely pushed me, but my next adventure would be the true test.

On the last day of the trip before I returned home, my team and Erik's team were going to summit my first 14,000 foot mountain (also known as a fourteener in Colorado) together, Mount Sherman. We started off that morning at 3 am, and started hiking around 6:00 am. Between the snow on the path, the rocky terrain, my fear of falling of the mountain, and the fact that I am pretty slow, we didn't know if we were actually going to summit that day because thunderstorms would be coming, and we needed to get down safely before they did. Thankfully we made it up, but again as Erik says the true summit is when you are back down safely.

But before we descended back down, we had a small celebration at the summit. No Barriers was doing a Pie it Forward challenge where people pledged to donate money and take a pie in the face, so I thought for publicity it would be great for Erik to pie me on top of my first fourteener. It went over well, and thankfully he didn't miss, but after the pie and lunch it was getting later in the day and we needed to start working our way back down fast. Not too far down from the summit, all hell broke loose. It started hailing, thundering, and there was so much electricity in the air that all metal, including the trekking poles in my hands, started shocking me, and making popping noises. My guide screamed at me to drop the poles, grab on to his pack, and run. During the rush I fell multiple times before they had me start sliding on my butt. I was scared, even starting to tear up at one point. The thought of Robert getting struck by lightning because he was the one helping me down motivated me to keep going. After many rocks hitting my butt, including one that ended up where no rock had ever gone before, I was at the end of my rope. Robert wanted me to try and shift to a reverse bear crawl position so I didn't keep hurting my butt, and after falling on my face a few times I finally got the hang of it. Once I was moving a little faster, Robert and I reached the gully we were sliding towards, and we were at least a little safer. From that point we took a different and steeper root down through loose rock, where I ended up on my butt again and eventually ended up shredding my pants. After working through a lot of stress, falling on slippery rocks, and laughing about my ripped pants, we made it to the bottom, and eventually caught up with the rest of the team who had made it down already. The moral of that day was don't tempt fate. But on the bright side, Erik's team finally decided on my nickname, and I am now known as Master Shredder.

Overall my adventure was amazing and life changing like most of the experiences I have with Erik, but I would be lying if I didn't say I was excited to get home, see my dog who I had left for ten days with my parents, and sleep in my own bed past 8 am. Also, I was mentally ready to continue working with my trainer, and I was going to start working with someone to climb mountains in my area. Once I had a little time to rest for a day or two, I was right back into the thick of things. I was going to hike my first mountain in New York, and after what I did in Colorado I figured this wouldn't be much. I traveled to the Adirondacks, and I was going to hike Mount Cascade. That day we started pretty early, but not early enough. Although the altitude wasn't anywhere close to what I was dealing with in Colorado, the path was so messy, the routes were not clean, and the obstacles I encountered were the toughest that I had encountered in hiking by far. I underestimated this mountain. I ended up hiking for nine hours that day, which was great from a training standpoint, but we didn't end up summiting because we didn't plan for it to get dark, and after my Mount Sherman experience I didn't feel like tempting fate again.

Even though it wasn't the day I thought it would be I had some good laughs along the way. First, so many people walked past me not realizing I was blind, but the best was a guy who said "You are so lucky because you have trekking poles," which got my guide and me laughing. Second, when nature calls there is no preventing what must happen next, especially after 5 hours of fighting the urge of going to the bathroom. Thankfully my guide had some gauze pad with him, but I was so scared the entire time I was either going to lose my balance and fall in it or worse, go on myself. Luckily, the mission was accomplished with no problems, and looking back now I just laugh.

My first hike in New York didn't turn out like I thought, but it didn't stop me from moving forward, and before I got a chance to catch my breath I would be off again. Before I made my trips out to LA and Houston to attend additional LEAP and Presentation Power programs, I ended up traveling to Colorado to go on another adventure with Erik. No Barriers would be holding its What's Your Everest event the weekend before I originally planned to go out to LA, so I figured there was no way I was going to miss that opportunity. After some planning with Erik's team, everything was in place, and the next thing I knew I was back at Erik's house again. Then we were off to the Keystone Resort where the No Barriers event would be. To my surprise, Erik came up with the idea that I should speak at the event he was speaking at. He said my story was a true No Barriers story, and it was a story he thought the audience should hear. Although I was nervous and not sure how everyone else felt about that idea, I wrote out a speech for the event, shared it with Erik, and he thought it was perfect.

My first night at the What's Your Everest event was crazy. I walked around with Erik, met many different people in attendance, and continued to remind myself that I was actually going to be one of the guest speakers. Best of all, my idol was going to actually introduce me to speak.

After the cocktail hour and dinner, people finally began speeches, and the next thing I knew Erik was up at the microphone about to introduce me. Although I was nervous because I didn't want to let Erik down, I ended up giving a great speech. That night was something special, and then next morning I hiked my fourth mountain, Dercum Mountain.

On top of planning with Erik's team to make coming out to this event possible, another key player in this was my Uncle Bob. It just so happened that he had a condo in Keystone, and he also would be on vacation while I was out in Colorado. The morning of the hike we met up, and that day my uncle would be my guide for the trek. The climb was honestly the easiest mountain I had done so far, and together we reached the top after 7 miles of hiking. It was another great feat for me to have accomplished, and it was the first summit I had experienced with any of my family members.

Although the event was over, I wasn't flying out to LA to meet my father for two more days, so once I had said my thank yous and good-byes to Erik and his team I went to my uncle's condo where I spent the next two nights. On the last night I got packed and ready to leave on the shuttle that was going to bring me at 5 am to the Denver airport to start the next part of my journey, and the next morning off I went.

My mother was all worried about me getting to the airport on my own safely, so I reminded her she would really have to prepare herself for when I hiked Kilimanjaro if that scared her, but the shuttle service I used and the people at the airport couldn't have been better. After a nice rest on the plane I met up with my Father at LAX. Now although I wasn't stressed, my father was a little out of his comfort zone, and after walking around forever, finding luggage, getting the rental car, and using my phone as a GPS, we arrived safely at the hotel.

I was going to LA to attend another LEAP program, but unlike the past where I was a student, this year I was one of the speakers. The best part was Jonathan Sprinkles was going to introduce me, which I was ecstatic about. It meant I was introduced by Erik and Jonathan in the same week!

My father and I arrived in LA on a Monday, and I wasn't speaking until Thursday, so we got to enjoy some of the area while we were there. We went to the Santa Monica Pier, where I played a popping balloon game with beanbags and won a prize for my mother. We visited a lot of iconic restaurants in the area including the famous In-N-Out Burger, Barney's Beanery, and Fat Sal's. We went swimming in the Pacific Ocean right outside of our hotel the first night. And we toured the UCLA campus. Also, while I was in Colorado I had been asked to speak for students attending the same pre-college program for the blind that I attended at Le Moyne. They even offered to pay me for speaking, and I figured it was a great opportunity. So while my dad drove around California sightseeing I conducted my calls.

Before I knew it, the day had come for me to speak at LEAP. Jonathan set the bar high with his own speech, so I had a lot to live up to.

I ended up doing great, the audience went wild, and my dad even said it was impressive because he didn't know how I was going to get up and deliver a speech after what Jonathan had said. Although I was ecstatic, we had to leave right away for the airport to catch our flight to Houston, Texas or we were going to miss it. Although it was hectic getting back to LAX and returning the rental car, we made it on time for our flight, and embarked on the last part of our journey at Presentation Power.

Unlike when I had attended the conference in January, this time my dad was going with me as my guest. I was pretty tired at this point, but I was energized to learn more from my coach and move myself forward in my speaking career.

Even though I didn't really plan on speaking, the next thing I knew I was in a competition with other members of the Industry Leaders Group (ILG), who were being coached by Jonathan and later that night I found out that I had been voted to speak by two votes. Don't get me wrong, I thought this was great, but I didn't have any dress clothes with me because I hadn't planned on speaking, so my dad and I needed to figure out how to get the collared dress shirt that I wore at LEAP cleaned so I could wear my suit again. Thankfully they had a laundry service in the hotel.

The second day was as good as the first, and I learned so much to implement into my speaking in the future, but by the end of the day I hit exhausted. Everyone in the ILG program were going out to dinner, including my friend Stuart and John who also were members of the LEAP program, so that gave me the energy I needed to push through. We had a great dinner together, and spending a night with Jonathan was a real treat.

When my dad and I returned to the hotel after dinner we were both ready to go to bed. But when we got back to the room to see if my shirt was in my closet like it was supposed to be, it wasn't there. After calling the front desk numerous times, they finally realized that no clothes had been picked up. Fortunately they agreed to have it personally cleaned that night, since I needed it the next day. At about 11:30 pm we heard a knock on the door and got a clean shirt back.

The next morning was hectic. After I was all dressed and ready to go, I was supposed to meet Robert in the lobby to discuss more about my MounTimPossible project, but because of some miscommunication we missed each other. After that I was stressed out because I had so little time, but everything worked out. I attended the conference in the morning, spoke at lunch, and then we got to work together for the remainder of the lunch period. To my surprise, Alex and his wife Amelia, who are also a part of the project and climbed Mount Sherman with me were there, and together we shot some video, worked out thoughts and ideas for the future, and the next thing I knew I was back in the conference room again to finish things up.

Once Presentation Power was over my dad and I headed out right away for our flight, and what would be the last part of my crazy trip. As usual it was a little insane getting from hotel to airport, but we arrived with plenty of time to spare. That night we returned home after my mom picked us up at 2:30 in the morning. Lang almost jumped out the window of the car when he saw me at the airport, and amidst a busy street with traffic I hand to calm down my dog, get him untangled, and finally back in the car so we could go home.

I passed out in my bed after watching a little bit of television to calm me down from everything that I had done over the last week and a half. In ten days I summited a mountain in Colorado, swam in the ocean, stood on the Santa Monica pier, spoke a total of seven times including being introduced by 2 of my biggest idols, attended one of the best conferences I've ever attended at Presentation Power, stayed in over six houses/hotels/condos, and ended up taking six different flights across the country, which included being in 2 of the 4 biggest cities in America. I was doing things I never could have imagined in my wildest dreams.

Chapter 5 It's Impossible Until You Do It

Now that you have gotten the opportunity to know me on a deeper level, the path I have traveled to get to where I am today, and why I am so passionate about what I do, I want to share with you the power behind *It's Impossible Until You Do It*. *It's Impossible Until You Do It* was my Make A Wish where I met Erik Weihenmayer and did things I never imagined possible for a blind cancer survivor. *It's Impossible until You Do It* was making it through my first semester of college with a 4.0; and *It's Impossible Until You Do It* was when I conquered the Grand Canyon. What *It's Impossible until You Do It* wasn't, was a destination.

So many times in our lives we are so focused on the destination that we forget what is truly important: the process. What made these moments so great in my life wasn't the fact that I did them, but that I did them despite others' views of me, including myself at times. That is what *It's Impossible Until You Do It* is. It is a mindset that you can conquer any barriers in your life even if others tell you it's impossible because you know the only one who has the power to place limits on you is yourself. Also, you never know if something is possible until you actually do it.

I thought completing the trek through the Grand Canyon was impossible, until I did it; I thought being successful at college would be impossible on my own, until I did it; and I thought being successful as a person who is a blind cancer survivor was impossible, until I did it. What these monumental achievements taught me and what I want to pass on to you is that the power to control your life is in your hands, not your circumstances. Now that doesn't mean my body will become super healthy all of a sudden or that I will gain my sight back tomorrow because I can't directly control those things, but what it does mean is I have the power to choose how I live my life. I can wallow in self-pity and think woe is me, or I can say this is what it is and enjoy myself as much as possible. As the saying goes, "Life is 10% what happens to you and 90% how you deal with it."

To help paint that image more vividly, picture if today were your last day left on this Earth. How would you choose to spend it? The answer is obvious for me, but I need to be honest and let you know it wasn't always. When I almost died from my cancer, I didn't choose to think I had control over my life, and I got rid of the power to do so by doing the one thing you can never do: give it to your circumstances. Although I would eventually get that power back, it wasn't an easy process, and once your circumstances have it, they aren't keen on giving it back. That is why I don't want you to make the mistake of giving your power away like I did. The following quote is the one I have found that sums this message up the best, and I wanted to make sure that I took the time to share it with you: "I can't choose how I die, but I can choose how I live."

I hope at this point you are filled with the same amazing feeling I had when I started to believe the power to control my life was in my hands, and realize circumstances in our life don't dictate our outcomes unless we let them, but this is only the halfway point. Although there are a lot of speakers in the world whose primary focus is to motivate, one thing I pride myself on doing is making a lasting impact on the people's lives I come into contact with. That is why I follow the equation Hope + Action = Success. I don't want to just be the person you heard speak and were inspired by, I want to be the person you heard speak and who helped you change your life by helping you live a fulfilled life from experiencing success on a higher level.

Hope can be defined as a strong belief in something you can't in many ways actually prove or quantify because it isn't actually tangible. One of the biggest examples of this strong belief in our society is religion. People believe if they do the right things when they are alive it will transfer over to experiencing a fruitful afterlife. People believe that there is an almighty all-knowing God who has a purpose for all of us even if we don't know what that is yet. People also believe God will never give us more than we can handle. The truth is, though, there is no real way of knowing other than having unquestionable faith, and that in essence is what hope is: belief in the unbelievable. As Little Elf Judy said in The Santa Claus movie, "Seeing isn't believing, believing is seeing."

When thinking of hope as a piece of a larger puzzle that ultimately results in the power to succeed, I think using an analogy is the best way for others to understand how each piece works together to create one highly functioning system. I have thought long and hard about what the best analogy would be to encompass everything I am offering in this book, and I believe attaining the power to succeed is like summiting a mountain. You can think of this mountain as the adversity we face in our lives that we are all capable of conquering. Hope in this case is the strong belief you have in the vision that you can make it to the summit, and it is this belief and motivation that is required to conquer any mountains in our lives. The reason you need hope or the belief that you can conquer mountains in your life to attain the power of success is because if you just have action without hope, then your results will be a failure to accomplish or follow through with anything you need to get done to reach your goal. That is why the equation for success is Hope + Action = Success.

If hope is the strong belief you have in the vision that you can make it to the summit, then action is everything you are going to need to do to get there. Action can be defined as the work you need to perform to achieve success, and it is crucial if you plan on reaching success in any area of your life. Without it, you just have hope. Hope alone is a recipe for disaster. It results in a lot of talk, big dreams, and things you want to do, but in the end, that is all it is because you never do anything to bring the vision you believe in so much to a reality.

Getting back to the analogy of climbing a mountain, here is what happens when you actually apply the formula for success. You combine the strong belief you have in the vision that you can make it to the summit with the work needed to be completed to make it to the top, and before you know it, you are standing atop the summit of a mountain in your life. Although I wish conquering the mountains in our life were as easy as me telling you the formula for success, I hope now that you at least believe success is in your grasp, and now all you have to do is go get it because, like anything great that people are able to accomplish in their lives, *It's Impossible Until You Do It.*

Having an idea now of where we've been and where we're going, including gaining the knowledge and hope that anything is possible, it is time to start taking some action. Action in this case is what I call embracing the ALIVE principles and that will be what you receive in the next five and final chapters of the book. They are a composition of all the knowledge and wisdom I have accumulated over the past seven years, and are personally what I do and have done to experience a fulfilling life in the face of my own adversity.

ALIVE is an acronym for the following principles, and just by remembering the letters you can always keep what you are about to learn close by. A stands for Adventure Outside of Your Comfort Zone. L stands for Live in Alignment with Who You Are. I stands for Incorporate Others in Your Life. V stands for View the World Optimistically. E stands for Experience the Life You Want To Live.

Before you continue on to the next five chapters I want to make sure that I am setting you up for success, and there are some things you should know on how to get the most out of each chapter before you do: a willingness to be open to new ideas, the desire to see through what you start and the discipline to actually put these principles into practice.

First, you must have an open mind. The principles lined out in the following chapters are not complex — most will seem intuitive — but if everyone were doing them, people would be much more fulfilled in their lives, which isn't actually the case. Also, maybe it is something you tried before and it didn't work for you when you did it that time, but it is important to remember that anyone who ever accomplished anything great started at or below the level you are at right now, and they didn't get to where they are by giving up, they actually just kept getting back up until they stopped falling back down.

Second, you need to have the desire to finish what you start. One way to actually test your desire is to ask yourself the following question. First, how bad do I want to be successful? If the answer is bad enough that you are willing to put in the time and effort to learn these principles and put them into action then you probably are ready. If not, remind yourself of what you won't be able to achieve if you choose to stay where you are. Every day we move forward or backward, so if you aren't moving forward, well, that means you must be going in the other direction, so make the conscious effort every day to move forward even if it is just one step. Eventually they add up.

Third, you need to have the discipline to apply what you learn in this book to your life. The good news is there will be a lot of opportunities to take little things away that you can apply, and eventually they start to add up and make a big difference. The bad news is if you don't take that first step toward putting these principles into action right away, chances are you never will, so make sure before you turn the page that you have the willingness to be open to new ideas, the desire to see through what you start, and the discipline to actually put these principles into practice.

Chapter 6 Adventure Outside of Your Comfort Zone

Adventuring Outside of Your Comfort Zone is the first principle we need to address in our journey towards living a life full of success in the face of adversity. This is crucial because it is all about taking that initial step, and without ever taking any steps towards what you want in life you won't be going anywhere. *Adventuring Outside of Your Comfort Zone* involves being able to master three skills: taking the first step, seizing opportunities that are placed in front of you, and becoming a lifelong learner. Alone, each of these principles will help you grow and become more successful in your life, but the true results come when you use them together.

Have you ever struggled with following through when you say you are going to do something? Have you ever missed out on opportunities in your life that you wish you had taken? Have you ever been in a situation where you wanted to do something but didn't know how? If you can say yes to any of these questions—and I know I have personally answered yes to all of them—then being able to adventure out of your comfort zone is exactly what I think you need. It won't be instant success, but since applying this principle in my life I have been able to see significant results and I am positive that you can too.

To help you understand more clearly the role that *Adventure Outside of Your Comfort Zone* can play in your life, I want to bring it back to the mountain climbing analogy. As mentioned before, action is the part of the formula of success that encompasses everything that gets you from deciding to climb a mountain, all the way to the summit, and back down safely. The five ALIVE principles are each a part of that process from start to finish, and if that's true then *Adventure Outside of Your Comfort Zone* can best be represented as part of the three-step process of making it to base camp.

Making it to base camp is the first step required to ascending a mountain, but there are a lot of things needed to reach that point. First, you will need to take action by making the decision to start learning everything you will need to know to have a successful climb. Second, you will need to start training and making yourself as strong as possible so you are prepared to do everything it will take to make it to the top. Third, you need to build up a team of supportive and successful individuals who share the same desire and vision that you do—summiting a mountain.

Though all three of those criteria are requirements of what it will take to make it to base camp, this chapter will focus directly on the need to take action by making the decision to start learning the things needed to have a successful climb. In essence, that is what it means to *Adventure Outside of Your Comfort Zone*, and I will now give you the skills so that you can do it in your life as well

Taking the First Step

The biggest problem we all face when it comes to getting anything done is the first step. It is the hardest to take many times, but if it is neglected, you will never be able to change anything. Luckily, by picking up this book, you have already made the first step towards the power to succeed in your life despite your circumstances. You know you are capable of doing it already, but for other areas in your life that first step may not be that easy. The benefits are abundant though, and instead of living a life of words and not actions, you will be using your newly acquired power to start off on the process to achieve anything you want in life. Also, once you have taken that first step, the others become easier and easier, and eventually you start building up a momentum that makes it impossible for setbacks to stop you in your tracks.

When it comes to taking the first step in any task you undertake, most of the time there is one thing preventing you from doing so. That thing is our enemy. Its name is fear. We all have fear in our lives but until we conquer it, we won't be sure that we can always make that first step and ultimately *Adventure Outside of Our Comfort Zone.*

The largest fears that I believe we all face are the fear of failure and the fear of the unknown. A fear of failure is the result of self-doubt and a fear of the unknown is the result of external factors in your life that you can't control. In either case, these fears can be destructive. However, the good news is that they no longer have to be the reason you aren't able to take that first step in all situations because I have some strategies for fighting back.

The first way people can conquer their fears is by getting comfortable with the uncomfortable. If our fears make us feel a particular way and prevent us from moving forward, then it seems logical that if we don't let our fears let us feel a particular way, then we won't experience them. Now this doesn't mean you can just flick a switch and you will be comfortable with fear instead of uncomfortable, but by training ourselves to become more comfortable with fear, the little steps outside of our comfort zone can become more frequent. Eventually those steps will get larger and easier to make because like anything you practice, you get better and better with time. Besides, keep in mind that what we fear isn't actually as bad as we make it out to be. Almost all of the things we waste our time worrying about never end up happening, and for the small amount that do, most of the time it is a lot less worse than we imagined it being.

The different ways you can step out of your comfort zone are numerous, and you know you are doing the right thing if you are a little uncomfortable and really pushing yourself to do that thing. One example is having a difficult conversation with someone who you are afraid will blow up or who may never want to talk to you again if you do. It won't be easy, but this is one way you can start making little steps out of your comfort zone. Another way is by striking up a conversation with someone you don't know. Not only will you be more comfortable with making conversations with people, but you will find that you will get to meet a lot of interesting individuals as well. A third way to step out of your comfort zone is by letting someone know how you truly feel about them. Whether you really like them, feel uncomfortable around them when they do something, et cetera, this can not only help you improve your relationships by making them more transparent, but your confidence of stepping outside of your comfort zone will grow tremendously as well. Whatever approach you use, always make sure you are not stepping out of your comfort zone with the intention to make others feel bad, stepping out of your comfort zone in a situation that isn't safe, or stepping out of your comfort zone if you are not ready to make that large of a step yet. Eventually those big steps will come, but like anything in our lives, it takes time.

Although stepping outside of your comfort zone is a way to take on all fear in your life, I think the next two strategies for doing so attack each of the two categories of fear I mentioned more directly. First, when it comes to tackling a fear of failure there is something you can do, and that is to embrace it. I know you might have just read that line again to make sure I said what I did, but we need to learn to embrace failure for what it is: a learning experience.

True failure is only when you fail, or, in this analogy, fall down and are unable to get back up without learning anything. If you know you can gain something every time you fall that will make you stronger when you get back up why would you fear it? Also, you won't be the first person in the world who has ever failed from anything. I know in many scenarios we think we are unique and no one knows what we are going through, but the truth is even the most successful people in the world have failed before if you ask them. The reason they became successful was because they learned from their failures, and when you do that you turn failures into learning experiences. So don't fear failing, embrace learning opportunities and remember that failure is only failure when you don't learn something from it.

The second strategy is to become more courageous, and it directly deals with our fear of the unknown. One of the things I need to be honest with you about is that just because you become more comfortable outside of your comfort zone and begin to treat failure for what it is—a learning opportunity—that doesn't mean fear will ever be completely removed from your life. We are people and we naturally get scared in different situations

65

where we are uncomfortable, and although embracing the first two strategies will help you tremendously, we never know when something is going to catch us off-guard. We need to be prepared to handle fear in those situations. The best way to do that is to become courageous.

Becoming courageous is, in a lot of ways, a chicken before the egg scenario. You need courage to overcome your fears, and by overcoming your fears you gain courage. The good news is that people throughout history have shown themselves to be courageous, so even if overcoming your fears makes you more courageous, you already have some inside you to work with or no one would ever be able to exhibit this quality.

There are three ways to become courageous, and although the first two will be talked about in Chapter 7 "Live in Alignment with Who You Are" and Chapter 8 "Incorporating Others in Your Life," I will include them here in minor detail as well. First, be confident in yourself. When you believe in yourself and know you have the ability to be successful in any situation, then you tend to not fear situations you are placed in. Second, surround yourself with a strong support network because sometimes we need other's to help us see the courage we have inside that we can't see ourselves — sometimes fears are too big for anyone to confront on their own. Third, and the strategy that will be primarily focused on in this section, is realizing fear doesn't have to be the thing that stops you. Everybody, including me, faces fear in their lives, but the difference with people who are able to overcome that more regularly than others is that they act in the face of their fears. It isn't easy to act in the face of your fears, but nothing worth doing in life ever is, and just because it isn't easy doesn't mean we give up and never strive to do it. This matters even more when you are in the face of adversity.

Could the worst possible thing happen to you when you act despite your fear? Yes, but there is still one chance that you could have the best outcome in your life, and that is the piece you need to focus on. I call this strategy the power of one because even if there are one million reasons why not to do something, as long as there is one good reason and you focus on that, it will be enough to get you through. I believe Nelson Mandela puts it best. He says, "I learned that courage was not the absence of fear, but the triumph over it. The brave man is not he who does not feel afraid, but he who conquers that fear."

Even though knowing what prevents people from stepping outside of their comfort zone and knowing how to confront fear are both very important to understand before you can move forward, there is one more thing I want to include in this section because I believe you need to hear it. What if today was your last day? How would you act? Would you sit back and let it just pass you by, or would you make the most of it because it is all you have left? Having been there before and not embraced this mindset, I don't want to ever be there again, and that is why I am sharing this with you now. Don't wait to get told you might die before you decide to start living every day like it is your last. I am sure when you thought about your last day alive in your head you did things you thought you would never do, but why then and not now? Any of us could die at any minute of any day, and even if it isn't tomorrow, we all have a limited time on this Earth, so don't waste it. Do the things you want in your life, don't let fear hold you back, and do them now while you still can. Why put off today what you don't know if you will ever get to actually do tomorrow? Most of all, take the time to join me in embracing this mindset because we all deserve to live a fulfilling life, especially when it is right within our grasp, and it doesn't matter what circumstances we face in our lives.

Seizing Opportunities

Have you ever felt that other people were just lucky and that's why they are successful? Do you think only opportunities go to rich people because they know other rich people? Have you ever felt you are just not meant to be successful? Well if you have accepted any of these myths, I want to let you know that they are just that—myths, and it is as simple as that. There might be some instances where they could be true, but is important to remember these three things: that while they may appear to be true, you don't really know what it is like to be in their shoes; it probably isn't long lasting; and just because there are exceptions in life doesn't mean the rule doesn't hold true. Anyone who has experienced long lasting success in their life can tell you it is because of their diligence, and their ability to seize opportunities that come about in their life. The good news is that any one of us can seize opportunities, no matter what background we come from, and I want to provide you with the tools to be able to do so.

The main reasons why people don't end up getting to take advantage of opportunities are a lack of seeking them out, being unprepared when they do, and failing to make the decision to accept them and follow through on them. I am going to address all of these, but I want to discuss some of the benefits that will come from being able to do all three. First, when you know how to seek out opportunities you will be overwhelmed in how many are out there, how many were sitting right in front of your face that you didn't even recognize, and how it didn't matter who you were because you were getting them regardless. Second, when you are prepared for opportunities it means that you have done what it takes to get them and take advantage of them, which means you have become a stronger individual. Third, when you are able to be decisive you will know right away what opportunities to accept, and won't miss out on any life changing ones because you were indecisive and waited too long. One of my favorite quotes on opportunities is by Leonard Ravenhill: "The opportunity of a lifetime must be seized within the lifetime of the opportunity" - which couldn't be truer because we can't sit back and let life's opportunities pass us by.

The simplest way to find opportunities in your life is by actively seeking them out. They are everywhere, so if you decide to actually start looking, listening, and feeling for them, you will be shocked with what you will find. To do this you first need to have a strong desire to find opportunities. Even more than that, have a strong desire for a specific outcome you want from an opportunity in your life. It is weird, but when you can actually picture so clearly what you want in your life, the world has a funny way of shifting to bring that image into a reality.

Another way to seek out opportunities is through getting to know and connect with others. If you want an opportunity then make sure you are talking with people about what you are looking for. You never know who they are and what doors they could open for you.

A third way to seek out opportunities, and probably the most important, is to keep your ears and eyes open to them. Most of the time this will mean being in tune with your surroundings and how you can best position yourself to find what you are looking for, but there is also an internal factor to this as well. If your body, mind or spirit is sending you messages, whether it be through happiness, pain, or dreams, don't just take them for granted. Sometimes we know more than we think, and being in tune to our senses is a very important piece of being aware of opportunities in our lives.

Once you have sought out opportunities, and hopefully now you know how to find them, the next step is actually being prepared for them. Do you know what you will say when the opportunity presents itself? Are you strong enough in the area of your focus to prove your abilities to others under any circumstances? Are you confident when it happens that you are ready? There are so many questions you could ask yourself, but the most important thing is that no matter what the opportunity is, you are ready. Whether that means practicing what you are going to do before it happens, getting to a level even stronger than you need to be to insure others will see you in a favorable light, or believing no matter what situation you are thrown into you can do it, you have to be ready. It is bad enough when you can't find opportunities, so be prepared for when you do. Nothing is worse than knowing you had a chance, and you weren't ready for it so you missed it. Good things come to people who are prepared for them, so keep those great opportunities coming by being ready.

At this point, we'll assume you found an opportunity to take advantage of, you have prepared doing whatever was necessary to get the most out of the opportunity when it presented itself, but now you need to determine whether to take advantage of the opportunity or pass on it. Fear sometimes can keep us from making a decision, but luckily we addressed that in the last section so you should be ready to confront that. What we didn't address yet is self-doubt and a lack of confidence. This will be heavily emphasized in the next chapter "Live In Alignment with Who You Are," but know that to be decisive, you need to be confident.

Knowing that decision making requires courage and confidence, the next problem is that you only have a limited amount of time to accept an opportunity before it goes away forever. That is why being decisive requires the ability to make decisions promptly, which comes with courage and confidence. By not having those qualities, most of the time you will never take advantage of opportunities, or in your hesitation because you are unsure what to do, you may pick a bad one. If you are feeling like you are at the point where you are all set to make a decision after doing your research but are still hesitant, remind yourself of the following quote by famous hockey player Wayne Gretzky: "You miss 100% of the shots you don't take." How very enlightening for those types of situations.

It is now time for you to start being lucky. You have the knowledge to attract opportunities to you, how to be prepared for them when they come up, and how to be decisive in taking advantage of them. The greatest success people have ever experienced has been just one step beyond the familiar. So if you arrive at uncertainty when taking advantage of a great opportunity, remember: be courageous, be confident, and you will never succeed if you never take any steps out of your comfort zone.

Being a Lifelong Learner

Taking the first step and seizing opportunities are both keys to being able to *Adventure Outside of Your Comfort Zone*, but the last of the three pieces, and one I really feel is the most important, is being a lifelong learner. Although the first two pieces are tough, bring on their own challenges, and can hold someone back from success in their life, being a lifelong learner is the toughest. I believe this is the toughest because the first two pieces deal with knowing things will be alright and having confidence, where being a lifelong learner means you have to accept the fact that you aren't the best, that you don't know everything, and that you are no better than anybody else. This is called experiencing true humility, and most successful people understand it, but it isn't the easiest quality to embrace or come by in others. Also, even though it may not be second nature to all of us to be truly humble and embrace what it means to be a lifelong learner, this is one area you will need to master to be successful. It is the only way you will gain the knowledge to take correct action, and here are some of the ways you can do that.

1. Develop an open inquisitive mind. The biggest barrier to achieving this mindset is arrogance. Arrogance is believing we know everything, believing our way is the best all of the time, and believing we are better than others. It is detrimental to many things in life such as personal growth and relationships, but in this case it specifically prevents you from learning. Without being able to learn, you will never have the ability to make informed actions. The good news is that there are things in your life that you can do to counteract arrogance, and here they are.

First, always remember that you would never be able to have what you value so much in your life if it weren't for the efforts of others. Everyone was a baby once, and unless you were different from all of the other babies in the world I have encountered, you probably had somebody who changed your diapers and fed you because you couldn't do it yourself. I am assuming you are little older now, so a more relevant analogy may be looking into the food you eat when you are out at a restaurant. Did you grow it? Did you transport it to the store and then to the restaurant? Did you cook it and deliver it to your own table? For most people that would be a big no, and although we don't really think about things like this every day, by remembering that we couldn't be where we are today without others, we can work on keeping our ego in check.

Second, be willing to accept information from anywhere. Now that doesn't mean take advice about how to handle your money from the person who bankrupted their last business, but it does mean that no matter who someone is, rich or poor, they can have valuable information to share. Dale Carnegie wrote "Everyone is your superior in some way." This couldn't be truer. Never let your arrogance get in the way of taking in valuable information from a source because you think it is incapable of providing it. Another way of looking at this is by following the time-tested principle, "Don't judge a book by its cover."

Third, realize that there is so much out there that you don't know. When you think about it, successful people aren't successful because they know everything. They are successful because they know a lot about something. The reason they know so much about something is they realize that they don't know everything and they never will know everything there is to know about their area of success. They were also open to others' opinions because they realized theirs were not perfect and could always improve. As the saying goes "Any man talks because he wants to say something, but a wise man talks because he has something to say."

2. You need to be excited about learning. People who are successful and very knowledgeable didn't get that way by thinking "I need to learn" — they got that way because they wanted to learn. Realize that learning is not a chore, but a privilege we have. To be able to be excited about learning, you need to develop an unquenched hunger for it. Honestly pick something you want to know more about, are interested in, or care about a lot, and just let yourself learn as much as you can about it. Eventually you will have mastered what you have been studying. It has been said that any subject studied 30 minutes a day for 5 years makes one an expert on that subject. I don't know about you, but the idea of being an expert at something really motivates me to learn more. If you want to know how I have learned everything I have included in this book other than from my personal experiences, it was through a hunger to be the strongest person I could be combined with a hunger to bring you the best book ever.

3. You need to be a good listener. We were given two ears and one mouth for a reason, and it was in hope that we would use them proportionately. Also keep in mind that if you rearrange the letters of listen you get the word silent. This makes so much sense because if we are speaking, then we aren't learning anything from someone else. If you give others the opportunity to talk they will because that is just human nature. But if you are running your mouth you aren't ever giving them a chance. Getting others to talk isn't the only piece; you need to stay attentive and keep your ears open. If you aren't, imagine all of the valuable knowledge you are missing out on. In addition, how do you feel when you are talking and people aren't listening to you? If you get frustrated like me, then why wouldn't you expect others to feel the same way if roles were reversed? Eventually that person will become so frustrated that they will probably no longer want to share their wisdom with you, and that is a point you never want to reach in a relationship. So embrace this principle by actually listening to what I have just said because this skill could be the difference that makes you or breaks you when it comes to success.

4. Ask questions. The saying goes you need to ask to get, and this is something I believe wholeheartedly. Sometimes the information we need to be successful is right there, but because we don't just ask for it, we never get it. The reason that successful people are successful is not just that they ask better questions, but because they also start listening as soon as the other person starts talking. In addition, they actually plan out the questions they are going to ask ahead of time. By doing this they know exactly what they want to get out of an interaction, and are sure not to forget anything important. Finally, successful people realize that a "no" isn't always a "no." Now this doesn't mean that you should repeatedly ask someone for something that they have refuse to give to you. However, what it means is that you can use a "no" as a learning opportunity to go back, see where you might have messed up, and if the situation seems like it could be successful after another approach, then do it. The worst you can get is another "no."

5. Know where to find knowledge. The most important piece to finding knowledge is knowing where to look. Although I will include a list of my top five sources I use to find information below, it is important to know one more thing before you try it. In order to be successful you should learn how to copy genius. The best way to become successful is to learn from others who are successful. For example if you want to be the best chef, you would probably want to learn from the best chef. There is no reason to reinvent the wheel — so many people try so hard to learn individually what another could have taught them in much less time. I want you to be successful not only in the future, but also as fast as possible. You will be well on your way by getting a hold of the sources I include below from people who have achieved success where you want to and people who you can look up to as role models.

My five sources are books, audio recordings, videos, successful people, and personal life experiences. The first three sources are great because you don't physically need a person to learn from right there in the room with you, and they don't require you to go out and experience anything. Although books can be tough because you need to sit down and actually read them, they are honestly one of, if not the best, ways to learn because they are compiled of the best knowledge authors have to offer. Audio recordings are great because even if it is an audio book, you can gain the advantage of learning without having to use your eyes. Now this isn't really a factor for me, but for those who drive or travel frequently it is a great way to learn on the go because you don't need to use your sight. In addition, videos are great because it is like having someone right there in the room teaching you. The only downfall is that you can't directly ask for questions if you have them, but that shouldn't be a reason for not using them.

The other two sources are successful people and personal life experience. In Chapter 8, "Incorporate Others in Your Life," I will discuss successful people more thoroughly with mentors and coaches. For now I will get right into the fifth and final source: personal life experience. As we talked about earlier in the chapter, failure is only failure if you didn't learn something from it. Although that was a negative experience, you can learn from your positive experiences as well. When you succeeded at something figure out how you did it, try and do it again, and work up to doing it that way all of the time. Your experience and personal judgement can be your greatest source of knowledge sometimes, so even though you should avoid thinking you know everything, make sure that you are pulling from your experience.

Now that you know how important listening and asking questions are, and know where to find knowledge, becoming a lifelong learner is right in your grasp. Again, it isn't easy, but the pursuit of knowledge is the thing that will separate anybody from being good and being great. The important thing to know though is that knowledge means nothing without action. The reason you are learning all of these things is so that you can apply them to your own life. Using this book as an example, I can help you and give you the tools to be the most successful person in the world, but if you never do anything with it you are no better off than the person who never learned it.

Summary

If you have reached this point you have almost completed your first chapter on the ALIVE principles, so give yourself a pat on the back. I'd do it for you, but chances are we aren't in the same room right now — but as discussed in the last section that doesn't mean you can't still learn something. You have now compiled the knowledge of how to be able to adventure out of your comfort zone by learning the three pieces required to do so, and I hope you are ready to take that first step, ready to seize opportunities, and ready to be a lifelong learner. Now that we have addressed how to adventure outside of your comfort zone, we can get into the other two principles that together will get you to base camp on your climb of the mountain of success. Before you do, however, I am going to provide you with a list of the ten most valuable points in this chapter that you can take the time to review later, and a personal story of how I have applied this principle to be successful.

Tim's Top 10: Adventure Outside of Your Comfort Zone

1. Get comfortable with being uncomfortable and be courageous in the face of your fears.

2. True failure is only when you are unable to learn and grow from it.

3. Live each day like it was your last and don't put off today what you might not get the chance to do tomorrow.

4. Seek out opportunities in your life and don't expect them to come to you.

5. Be prepared to act and follow through on opportunities when they present themselves.

6. Develop an open and inquisitive mind through embracing true humility.

7. Have an unquenchable hunger for learning.

8. Ask the right questions and listen closely when you get the answers you are looking for.

9. Know where to find knowledge and who the successful people are you should be getting your information from.

10. Knowledge is only power when you put it into action to get what you want in life.

Principles in Action

One example where *Adventure Outside of My Comfort Zone* literally changed the course of my life was when I attended the LEAP program at UCLA in 2014. I mentioned earlier in the book how this experience completely changed my life, but I want to let you know how I used the ability to *Adventure Outside of My Comfort Zone* to bring this experience into a reality, and what my life would be like if I never took this opportunity. Although it may seem backwards, the first thing that got me to attend this experience was from being a lifelong learner. Every chance I got, I was always looking up events at my college where I could become stronger, more knowledgeable, and more informed about things I knew nothing about, and it was that hunger that led me to find out about the LEAP program. A student had posted on Ithaca College's alert system about it, mentioning how this program completely changed her life, and on top of it all there was an option to apply for a scholarship to go for free. At this point, I embraced seizing the opportunity and I looked up more about the program so that I could make an informed but timely decision. Finally there was one thing that really pushed me over the edge and got me to submit my scholarship application. Unlike any program I had attended before, this program was comprised of some of the brightest minds from all over the world, and unlike me they were able-bodied. My fears of failure in not getting a scholarship and the unknown of other kids not liking me almost got the best of me, but I was urged by my supportive mother and internal drive to want to prove myself wrong — so that is exactly what I did. Not only did I apply, but I also got accepted, which would change my life forever.

By attending LEAP I made some of my best friends. I met mentors who have helped shaped me into the man I am today. I decided that the power to control my life was in my hands, not my circumstances. Most of all, it is where I brainstormed MounTimPossible, which is not only going to change my life, but the lives of so many others, and ultimately help the world redefine what they perceive as possible—just as I am trying to do with this book. Adventuring outside of my comfort zone honestly changed my life, and this is just one of many experiences where applying this principle made a big impact. There are so many more, and though they aren't all on that scale, they are still all important to my success. Even small things can make big differences.

Chapter 7 Live in Alignment with Who You Are

Living in Alignment with Who You Are is the next principle we need to address in our journey towards living a life full of success in the face of adversity. Without experiencing a mastery of who you are, the last three principles won't be easy to implement; this is especially true for Chapter 8, "Incorporate Others in Your Life." We need to be able to solve things from the inside before we can solve them on the outside. So instead of looking at how we can improve others, let's do what's in our control and improve ourselves first. *Living in Alignment with Who You Are* involves mastering three skills. The first is knowing who you are. The second is striving to be your best. The third is being confident in you. By being able to master all three of these skills you will become the person that you always were and were always meant to be. As a result you will be more fulfilled in your life than ever before, no matter what challenges you are faced with.

One of the biggest areas people struggle with is self-confidence. People don't know who they are or what they stand for; people don't know how to embrace what they have to become the best version of themselves; and people don't know how to deal with the negative and limiting opinions of others. I personally know how detrimental any of those thoughts can be, which is why I think that even if we are confident in ourselves there is always room for us to grow. If your circumstances have put you in a situation where you are experiencing any of these feelings, have hope because living in alignment with who you are could be the answer you have been looking for.

To help you understand more clearly the role *Live in Alignment with Who You Are* plays in your life, let's return to the mountain climbing analogy. As mentioned before, there is a three-step process for reaching base camp. In the previous chapter, we tackled the decision to start learning about how to have a successful climb. In this chapter we will address the next step, which is starting to train and making yourself as strong as possible so you are prepared to do everything it will take to make it to the top. After that we can officially move on to the third step of making it to base camp, which is building up a team of supportive and successful individuals who share the same desire and vision you do of summiting a mountain. But before we get to all of that, here are the skills that will guide you on the course of self-mastery.

Knowing Who You Are

Who are you? No really, who are you? Before you can move on to striving to be your best and being proud, you have to be able to answer this question, and for many people (including myself) there sometimes is no obvious answer. The good news is that the answer is there; sometimes we just have to dig deep to find it. Since I have been there before, I have developed a process to help us in digging for the inner you.

In order to answer the question of who we are, there are five precursor questions I have landed upon that we need to ask ourselves. Who are you at the most basic level? What are your strengths and weaknesses? What are you passionate about? What motivates you? What are your core values?

I've broken these questions down even more, into a 15-part assessment. I didn't have a guide when I was figuring this entire process out, and that is why I have taken everything I have learned throughout my process to craft this assessment for you. You might feel the urge to skip the next section without answering the questions. But if you really want to achieve personal mastery, there is no way around answering the question, "Who am I?"

The "Who am I?" assessment will begin on the following page and will conclude this section, but before you go on here are three things to keep in mind. First, be honest. If you lie the only one you will be fooling is yourself. You are the best possible you because that is the only person you are ever going to be, so why not try and get to know that person better instead of being a lesser version of someone else. Second, if you don't know look it up. Some answers may require more digging than others to reach, so taking what you learned in the previous chapter, use the different sources of learning to dig deeper for the answers that you can't find near the surface. Also, what may not appear clear to you is sometimes very apparent to others, so if you are struggling with your answers or are not sure what you put is right, ask the people closest to you what they think. Sometimes these people can help us see what we sometimes can't see on our own, and that is why having strong relationships is so important. Third, once you figure out who you are, become the best possible you. This is what the next section, which deals with personal growth, will be focused on. Just remember, you can't build on a shaky foundation, so take this assessment seriously, and then from there build yourself up.

"Who Am I?" Assessment

1. What is the origin of your name? What does it mean, how did you get it, etc.

2. What is your family like? Where do they come from, what traditions do you have, etc.

3. What part of your body do you like the most? Why that one, what about it makes it the most likable, etc.

4. What characteristic or skill is your strongest? Why is it your strongest, are you proud of it and want to share it with others, etc.

5. What characteristic or skill is your weakest? Why is it your weakest, are you ashamed of it and try to hide it from others, etc.

6. What is the one area in your life that if you took the time to improve it, would make the biggest difference in your ability to be successful? Why that area specifically, what is preventing you from improving it, etc.

7. What brings you the most joy in your life? Why are you so happy when you are doing this thing, what makes it more special than anything else that makes you happy in your life, etc.

8. What is the one thing in your life that if it were gone tomorrow, would almost make life not worth living anymore? Is it an activity you do, is it a person, animal or character you spend time with, etc.

9. What is the one thing in your life that you would give your life to protect? Is it loved ones, is it a vision greater than yourself, etc.

10. What gets you out of bed in the morning? Is it getting a fresh start, is it because you are working towards achieving something great in your life, etc.

11. What provides you with the most inspiration in your life? Is it another person, music, an inspirational story, what makes that so motivating, etc.

12. Who motivates you the most in your life? Is it a family member, a teacher, or a friend, what about them makes you motivated when you are around them, etc.

13. What are your top five core values? Why are these values so important to you, how did these values come to be the ones you cherish the most, etc.

14. What values do you appreciate in others? Why do you appreciate them so much, do you exhibit this value in your own life, etc.

15. Which value gets you the most worked up when you see another person violating it? Why does it work you up so much, is it something you do or just others?

Striving to Be Your Best

I hope the exam was insightful in learning more about who you are, and that with that information at your fingertips, you can start striving to be your best. Now, even though you know who you are, this doesn't mean that you are the best version you can be yet; we can all continue to grow no matter how strong we are in certain areas of our lives.

Striving to be your best shouldn't be limiting. Striving to be your best is accepting that you aren't going to get a new body, new mind, etc., so you need to work with what you have. It is also about knowing who you are, what you stand for, and allowing yourself to become your best without compromising those things. If you have a bad habit and that is who you don't want to be, then don't. If you have a weakness that you want to make a strength, do it. And most importantly, if there is something you can be doing in your life to make you more successful that you aren't doing, do it.

Even though I have compiled ways in which you can strive to be the best you, I want to point out two things before I get into them. First, personal growth is not easy, but it is the most rewarding process you will ever experience if you are willing to embrace it. You will need to be self-motivated and self-disciplined to see results, but these things are a small price to pay in becoming the best you. Second, don't expect instant gratification. Our society, in a lot of ways, is a place in which we seek the biggest rewards while putting in the smallest amount of effort — and that doesn't fly with personal mastery. To me, the best analogy I have come across is personal mastery is like a skyscraper. There is a lot that goes into it, including the work to create the blueprints etc., but at a certain point, you start building and showing growth externally. Then, before you know it, you are a towering skyscraper that everyone can't help but notice.

1. Use what you've got. One of the biggest reasons why people aren't able to grow or tackle the adversity in their life is that they are waiting for something to change, and they keep telling themselves they just aren't blank enough. That blank could be strong, that blank could be smart, or that blank could be rich, but by accepting any of those beliefs, you will never be able to grow. As I keep mentioning, no one great ever started off where they are now. Successful people are resourceful, and they don't waste their time thinking about what they don't have. Instead they focus on what they do have, and use that to grow and become successful. They also realize they are only going to have one body before they pass on, so they can either strive to make it the best it can be, or live a non-fulfilling life.

One of the easiest ways to think about using what you've got is by looking at the "Who Am I?" assessment from the last section. In the "Who Am I?" assessment, one of the areas you looked at was your strengths and weaknesses. Now that you have assessed what those are in your life, you need to start maximizing and minimizing.

Maximizing means you hone your strengths and make them your strongest assets. For example I was a good speaker, but by practicing, gaining more experience, taking in feedback, and ultimately maximizing my strength I was able to become a great speaker. We all have something in our lives we are good at, and once you are positive on what that is you need to bring that strength to the next level.

Minimizing is the other side of this coin, and it is in many ways more important than maximizing. When you maximize you are taking what you are strong at and fortifying it even more. But when you minimize, you are taking something that is holding you back and turning it into something that no longer holds you back. Minimizing is key for being successful in the face of adversity. For example, my blindness was one of my biggest weaknesses. Over time though, I learned how to make it nothing more than a different way of experiencing the world around me, and in many ways I have actually been able to turn it into an asset. As the saying goes "A chain is only as strong as its weakest link."

Now that you understand the idea that we only have what we are given in life, I hope you realize that the power to succeed is in your hands still. It's not where you start, it's where you finish, and the way to finish strong is to take what God has given you and get the most out of that in the time you have.

2. Be disciplined. Although there are a lot of things we can't control in our lives, there are many that we can, and most of them are things everyone can do regardless of who they are. The key is that they all focus on discipline. There are three types of discipline anyone can control in their life: the effort they put towards any task, the amount of practice they make to master a skill, and the level of integrity and character they hold themselves to. Again, the best part of all three of these disciplines is that anyone can master them. They do not lie out of our control, even though people often end up blaming their failure on them.

First, the effort you put into any task is something you have direct control over. Personally I would say give 100% of your effort towards anything you do, but I always think we can reach farther than what is perceived as possible, so I strive to give over 100%. This is a mindset that I believe you should adopt too. It is amazing how much we can get done if we use all of our effort to do it, and the quality of the final product tends to be much better as well. Although chapter 10 will address prioritization, know that giving everything you have is important, but directing that effort towards the most important things you need to get done in your life and nothing else, can lead you to even more amazing results. "What counts is not how many hours you put in, but how much you put in the hours."

Second, the amount of practicing you put in for mastering any skill is in your control. The saying goes practice, practice, practice, and that is because no matter what you want to achieve in life, you won't be able to do it without practicing it. Can some people do things without practice? Sure, but to be able to do that on a consistent basis and be confident in your ability isn't something that is going to come overnight. The concept of practice goes back to the idea of how *It's Impossible Until You Do It*, and how it's the process not the destination. All of the hours you are willing to put in are what matters and what you will remember in the end. The only one standing in the way of practicing what we want to be able to succeed in is ourselves, so ultimately the decision to become the best version of ourselves possible is in our hands, making us the person to blame if we don't. As William A. Ward once said, "Study while others are sleeping; work while others are loafing; prepare while others are playing; and dream while others are wishing."

Third, the ability to be a person of integrity and character is in our control. These are two traits I hope you hold close, and if not, you still will want to work on them as if they are because no one succeeds without some form of integrity and character. What you become is a lot more important than what you accomplish in life. In the end you may not have much to show for yourself, but wouldn't you rather be remembered as the person others couldn't say enough good things about than a person who had no values and experienced success? Nobody lacking character will ever succeed in a meaningful way, so why would you push off becoming a person of integrity and character if your goal is to truly succeed in life?

Five key values associated with integrity and character that you will need to adopt and practice in your life are honesty, authenticity, punctuality, self-control, and the ability to do the right thing even when no one else is looking. First, be honest. Tell the truth, set clear expectations with others, and remember honesty is always the best policy. Also, remember that honesty will go a long way with others in building trust, so if you want to be truly successful then be honest. Second, be authentic. If you believe you are acting fake, other people probably see it too, so just be yourself. Live with your heart on your sleeve, and when you say you are going to do something, do it. In a lot of ways, a person's word is really all they have in their life, so protect it with that level of importance because once you lose it, it is hard, if not impossible, to get back. Third, be punctual. You can't control how your next meeting goes, but you can control whether or not you are on time to it. Even though it is something very simple, most people aren't punctual, but by doing so you can show how important what you are about to do is to others, while also showing yourself that you have the discipline to do what you set out to do. Fourth, have self-control. As humans we let ourselves get rattled by others and the circumstances that arise in our lives, but to succeed we need to "Be proactive," as Steven Covey says in his first of 7 habits for highly effective people. We need to be patient, not let our emotions get the best of us in the moment, and not react immediately, but be proactive by reflecting on the situation and then choosing the best possible choice for moving forward and achieving the outcome we want. Fifth, do the right thing even if no one else is looking. It may be easier to to let this slide, but you need to realize that every time you do, you are more likely to exhibit those habits in front of others.

These five key values associated with integrity and character will take time to practice, like anything else. But at the end of the day, even if you don't see it right away or think they are important, these values will make the difference between experiencing success that isn't true and long lasting, and living a life full of meaningful success.

3. Learn to motivate you. One of the hardest skills we all need to learn is how to motivate ourselves. On days when we wake up and our ambition is low and it seems that the adversity in our life is getting the best of us, we need to be able to draw from the internal motivation; we have to strive to be the best we can be. Whether it is practicing a skill, a value, or just working on forming a new habit in your life, you need to be consistent and that comes with the ability to motivate yourself to do things, even when you think you don't want to. This motivation must come from inside and not externally because when you are in the moments where you are alone and don't have someone right there to push you forward you need to be able to do it yourself.

The two most important aspects of self-motivation are passion and a desire to succeed. First, think of your answers for the "Who Am I?" assessment when asked about passion and motivation. When you are doing those things in your life that make you feel happy, inspired, and give you a sense of purpose, they are motivators themselves. When you are passionate about doing something, you are willing to put in the effort and practice to be successful. In your worst times you have to draw from this passion and remind yourself why you are doing what you are doing in your life. By sourcing this passion, you can motivate yourself to continue on because you remember how important what you were doing was in the first place. I have also found that things like quotes, videos, music, and other things in my life are great ways of reminding me what motivated me to do what I am doing in the first place. Even though these are external sources, you have the control to surround yourself with these different forms of motivation. Even if it doesn't make sense to others, if it reminds you why you are motivated to accomplish what you want in life. Use anything you want to guide you in this process.

A desire to succeed is another strong motivator to help you in achieving success in the face of adversity. Not only do I want to succeed in my life personally to show myself I can achieve whatever I set my mind to, but I want to show others as well. Nothing motivates me more or gets me to do something I am not sure I can do than when someone says I will never be able to do it. Those words light a fire inside me, and the determination I have to succeed in those moments is unrivaled by anything else in my life. Even though they are strong feelings in the moment, the true power comes when we can harness that energy to pull from in the future. Sometimes you may think they are right and sometimes you may think you can't do it, but if you use that drive you initially felt to succeed when someone told you that you couldn't then amazing things happen. You gain the strength to keep going on, and eventually if you keep it up long enough you will gain the satisfaction of knowing it was impossible...until you did it.

4. Have a way of measuring growth. So far we have addressed using what you've got, being disciplined, and learning to motivate ourselves, but the last piece of this is to be able to measure how we are growing in all the areas we want to improve on in our lives. First, you have to assess where you currently are. Although there are a lot of ways to do this, I think the simplest and most effective way is to write down the areas in your life where you are successful, where you want to improve, areas that are important to you, etc. Then write a number one through ten next to it — number will be your base number, and your goal is to then work hard to bring all of those numbers up to a ten. Remember that you need to be brutally honest with yourself, and a 10 isn't always attainable.

We need to be brutally honest with ourselves. People tend to look at the negatives in others and the positives in themselves, but in order to grow and become stronger you need to start looking at things in the other direction. This doesn't mean you should tear yourself down, but if you aren't willing to accurately assess where you are then how can you assess how far you still need to go? If you rate yourself super high you may think you are perfect in that area, but as I will lie out, perfection isn't possible. Additionally, take the time to reflect on your scores every week. Include where you did well in each area, include where you messed up in that area, and then find out what you should do in the future to learn from your mistakes so you don't make them again. Failure isn't failure if you learn something from it, and by assessing your growth every week you can make sure that you are staying focused, moving in the right direction, and constantly determining what worked and what didn't so you can strive to be your best in the most efficient way. Although we can't control where we start our journey towards personal mastery, we can control where we end it.

One important thing to note about striving to be your best is that you can't just focus on your strengths. The whole idea of maximizing your strengths and minimizing your weaknesses comes into play here, but as I emphasized earlier, minimizing your weaknesses is more important than maximizing what you are already strong at. A good way to think about this is directing two-thirds of your focus towards weaknesses and one-third towards strengths. Doing this will not only insure that you become stronger in your strongest areas, but it will also keep your weaknesses from bringing you down drastically.

Remember, a ten isn't actually attainable. Everybody can always strive to become stronger in any facet of his or her life, so the idea that you can actually master something is not possible. What is possible is becoming the best person that you are able to. When you reach that next level of greatness, assess what there still is to learn or improve upon and keep building up. Always remember that even though perfection is unattainable, it doesn't mean we strive for it any less.

Striving to be your best will take some knowledge, discipline, motivation, and a good system for reflecting on your growth, but becoming the best "you" is one of the biggest ways we can achieve success in our lives no matter what comes our way. And now that we know who we are and how to strive to be our best, we need to now do what it takes to be confident in ourselves, and that includes the times when we may be the only one who is.

Being Confident in Yourself

Knowing who you are and striving to be your best are both important to *Liv in Alignment with Who You Are*, but if you lack confidence then you won't be able to share that person with the world. That means you won't be able to move on to mastering what is about to come in Chapter 8. People who lack confidence attack others verbally and physically because of their feelings of inferiority; they can't praise others for their success because they think it brings them down; they don't stay persistent to their personal growth because they don't believe they have the power in their hands to be successful in the face of adversity. All of these examples and more are detrimental in your journey towards a fulfilling life. Even though self-confidence requires a balance between believing in yourself and arrogance because you think you are better than everybody else, I know you are capable of doing it.

Some of the biggest enemies that stand in the way of you and self-confidence are comparing apples to oranges, negative influences, and criticism. This section will address all three of these enemies, and provide the tools you can apply in your own life to thwart them.

First, comparing apples to oranges. Do you ever find yourself comparing your accomplishments to others? I know I have, and not only does this either make me upset or send my ego on overload, but all of the emotion gets in the way of me actually seeing that they are an orange, and I am an apple. This is important because you can't be comparing yourself to people that you have nothing in common with. We are all unique and a population of one, so comparing yourself to others doesn't make much sense when you think about it. Regardless, we all do it. But to be confident in yourself you will need to fight our natural instinct and employ the use of measuring our growth with our own measuring stick and not anybody else's.

When measuring your growth with your own measuring stick it is important to remember the reason we can't measure with others is because in addition to having different experiences, we are also all at different spots in our life. As America's Ambassador of Hope, I constantly have to keep this in mind because although I am here now, I wasn't always, and I used to be in the spot some of you are at right now. So I have to remember what it was like when I first encountered adversity in my life to accurately understand how I can help you the most by thinking about how I would have helped myself.

Second, negative influences. If you want to question whether negative influences exist, go no further than a television, radio, etc. and listen for a couple minutes. No matter where we are it seems like we are always being inundated with negative influences from all over. I haven't even mentioned the other people we encounter in our life that put us down constantly, but I know we all know who those people are, and ignoring them doesn't make them go away. The person who said sticks and stones may break my bones but words can never hurt me must have been a robot because not only do they hurt, but negative words also plant seeds of doubt in our heads that, if left unchecked, grow into full-fledged plants.

Despite the negativity in this world, we can combat it by filling our mind with positive influences, and one way to do this is through self-affirmations. As the Chinese proverb goes "All the water in the world cannot sink a ship until it gets inside."

Self-affirmations are positive thoughts that you fill your mind as a result of repetitively encouraging yourself. The most amazing thing is after a while, just like negative influences, they plant seeds in your mind and grow until you have great trees of positivity that prevent seeds of negativity from growing there. Although it isn't easy to get these seeds to grow at first, because you will need some practice, when you have a vast forest of trees you will be glad you put in the initial effort.

Self-affirmations can come from any of the ways our senses take in stimuli from our surroundings, but for me personally I find saying something out loud does the best. Imagine you don't like the way you look, which after everything my body went through I struggled with a lot. Instead of letting that become the way you think about yourself, wake up every morning, look in the mirror if you can, and tell yourself you are beautiful. It may take a while, but eventually after telling yourself over and over again the outcome you will start believing in the result you want to see. This can work in any scenario of your life. Tell yourself you are going to succeed, tell yourself the power to control your life is in your hands not your circumstances, and tell yourself *It's Impossible Until You Do It*. I believe your results will shock you, and your confidence won't just contribute to your personal growth, but also in your ability to bring your visions into a reality as well. You need to see it to be it, so until you can convince yourself of your vision of what you want, chances are it will never manifest into its physical form. But watch out, because when you do, the ability to turn your thoughts into reality will give you exactly what you have been looking for succeeding in the face of any adversity.

Third, criticism. I imagine I am not alone when it comes to disliking criticism, and that is because there really is no good form of positive criticism except constructive feedback. But if we think we will escape life without receiving it, we are dead wrong. As you become more successful you will attract more critics, and although that is a good sign that things are working, if you aren't prepared to handle all of this criticism then you will be in a bad position to stay confident in yourself. That is why I want to provide you with tips on how to remain positive in the face of criticism, how to best receive it, and how to assess its relevancy.

Criticism shouldn't be looked at as an enemy we should run away from, but a friend who is going to help us get to where we want to be. Although some people might deliver criticism with the worst intent, by examining it we can take at least something positive from it to apply to our lives, even if that wasn't the person's intention. If you don't believe me then try it out. The next time you receive criticism, embrace it. Don't react like you normally would by defending yourself, denying anything happened, or avoiding it completely. Instead take it and then try to apply what you have learned to your life. See how much stronger and more composed you are as a result.

Although it is important to embrace criticism, not all criticism should weigh on you as much as others. If a friend criticizes you, you can assume that they have your best interest at heart. However, if it is a stranger that is giving you criticism and has no idea what goes on in your life, then the criticism shouldn't weigh on you too much; they were probably just someone in a bad mood trying to bring another person down to their level. When trying to figure out how to handle criticism I have discovered three ways that have helped me and they are as follows. Evaluate who said it, evaluate how well they actually understood what they were criticizing, and after assessing the validity of it, respond to it properly instead of reacting in the moment. Taking all three of these methods into account, you no longer have to feel that you don't have the control to handle the negative things others say about you. Now you can turn them into positive ways to become stronger and know only to accept criticism from those you determine fit to give it.

Summary

You have almost finished Chapter 7 on living in alignment with who you are, and now it's time to start using what you learned in this chapter to become the strongest version of yourself. Through knowing who you are, striving to be your best, and being confident in yourself you can start to become the confident and successful person you were always meant to be. When you are at your personal best you are ready to start incorporating others in your life, and that is what you will learn in the next chapter. But before you go on, make sure to check out the most valuable lessons of this chapter in the list of the top 10 points below. Then check out how I have used this principle in my life to grow to be confident and successful because like everybody else, I started probably at or farther down than where you are now. This gives me all the hope in the world that you can use this principle to be successful in the face of your adversity too.

Tim's Top 10: Live in Alignment with Who You Are

1. Discover who you really are

2. Get the most out of what your body has to offer because you only get one

3. Give 110% effort towards anything you do

4. Practice is the only way you will become great at anything

5. Be a person of integrity and character even when no one is looking

6. Learn how to motivate yourself when you need it the most

7. Consistently measure your growth using a system that works for you

8. Strive for perfection in anything you do even if it is unattainable

9. Use self-affirmations in your life

10. Embrace criticism

Principles in Action

One example where living in alignment with who I am made a difference was during my trek through the Grand Canyon in 2014. At this point, I was new to the adventuring world, and even though I was leaps and bounds above where I was when it came to my strength since my long stay in the hospital, I still had a long way to go to being what I considered strong again.

When I got the opportunity to go on this journey through the Grand Canyon I was thrilled. Ever since meeting Erik Weihenmayer on my Make-A-Wish, I wanted to be an adventurer just like him, and this was my biggest opportunity to do just that. The problem was that I wasn't ready physically when I received the opportunity; others doubted that I was strong enough to do it and eventually, all of the negativity in my life transferred over to me believing I couldn't do it myself.

By taking the time to remember who I truly was at heart, motivating myself to train hard because I believed in myself and wanted to prove others wrong, and filling myself with positivity and confidence that I was going to succeed, I decided to take on this monumental feat. The four days on the rim of the canyon took some getting used to with camping outdoors for the first time ever over multiple days, the seven days on the river pushed me to my limits physically, but nothing was like the hike I completed out of the canyon on the nine and a half mile Bright Angel Trail. Although I kept my positive mindset, the negative thoughts dripped back into my head of people saying I wasn't strong enough to do it. I battled hard, I thought many times of just giving up, but all of my practice prepared me for what I needed to do. And after thirteen and a half hours I accomplished what I thought was one of the hardest things in my entire life.

This personal mastery of knowing who I was even in the face of adversity, getting myself to become the best using the body I was given, and being confident in the face of negativity are what propelled me forward. They are the same things that, when you master them in your own life, will propel you forward too. I hope you realize the power behind this principle, and with enough due diligence you will be taking on the mountains in your own life.

Chapter 8 Incorporate Others in Your Life

Incorporating Others in Your Life is the third principle you have to address to continue on your journey towards success in the face of adversity. The reason why it is so important is because it involves one of the biggest universal truths of life. That truth is nothing great was ever accomplished by anyone on their own. Once you can see how much you need others in your life, how having others in your life is one of the greatest feelings you can ever experience, and how by helping others you can change lives, you will be equipped to take on some of life's hardest challenges.

Like all of the principles in this book, there are three skills you will need to master before you can master the principle itself. For incorporating others in your life, these skills are some of the most important in the entire book. They are communicating effectively with others, surrounding yourself with the right people, and living a life of service. All of which can make the difference between a life full of success and a life full of mediocrity

Everyday people struggle with how to interact with others, who their friends really are, and whether they should help others succeed in their lives. I don't want you to struggle any longer in these areas, and the impacts from developing these skills in your life will be tremendous. True success in life comes when you experience success with others, so in order to experience true success pay close attention here.

To help you understand more clearly the role which incorporating others in your life plays, I am going to use the mountain climbing analogy again. It may be hard to believe, but at this point we are already only one step away from reaching base camp. We have learned how to take action by making the decision to start learning about everything we need to know. We have learned how to start training and making ourselves as strong as possible so we are prepared. And now we just need to learn how to build up a team of supportive and successful individuals who share the same desire and vision we do of summiting a mountain. This step is what you can accomplish when you master incorporating others in your life, and get ready because it is these skills that have changed my life so much, and I know can do the same for you.

Communicating Effectively with Others

Building and maintaining relationships are core aspects of succeeding in life, and building relationships is all about one thing—effective communication. Your ability to effectively communicate creates a foundation upon which friendship of all levels can be built, and that is why I want to help you master this skill. Most people have no idea of just how much power resides in what they say and how they say it, but what we say and how we say it can have a life changing impact on others.

There are three areas that together lay a strong groundwork for mastering effective communication, which translates over to helping people build and maintain relationships. They are making people feel important, being an active listener, and handling arguments. Being able to master all of these skills will not only help you build relationships, but they will help you improve the ones you already have.

Before moving on it is important to remember at the core of everything discussed in this chapter is the golden rule, which is treat others the way you want to be treated. Whenever you say something or do something think to yourself, *is that how I would like someone to say or do that to me?* If you wouldn't than why are you doing it to someone else? Keeping this rule in mind is a good gauge for whether what you are saying or doing is the right thing or the wrong thing. Also, in order to build relationships you will always need to be thinking about what you are going to say or do next, so add this to the list of things to keep in mind while reading the three steps.

1. Make people feel important. As sad as it is, we all know what it is like to not be accepted, excluded from a group, or made to feel worthless in our lives. It makes us upset, it makes us angry, and it can lead to low self-esteem. Knowing how we

feel in these situations, it is important to always try not to put others in that same scenario. Instead do the exact opposite by making them feel like they are the most important person in the world. Not only will you shock people with how special you make them feel, but by communicating how much you care about someone you are planting the seeds to form a long lasting relationship in the future.

Dale Carnegie says "We should picture everyone we meet as wearing an invisible sign around his neck saying make me feel important." Keeping this in mind, I have developed three ways in my life to fulfill that role of making others feel important. The first will be discussed in Chapter 9 and deals with appreciation and giving praise and encouragement where it is due. The other two, which will be discussed in this section, are treating everyone like a rock star and addressing people by their name.

First, if you want to make people feel important then treat them like they are important. For me this translates over to treating everyone you meet like a rock star. Imagine if your favorite celebrity walked in the room. How would you act, what would you say? Now imagine if we acted this way towards everyone we met or had an existing relationship with. Don't you think others would be shocked? When you are able to make people feel special, they want to get to know you better, they act extremely nice around you, and eventually it could turn into a relationship.

It isn't hard to treat others like they are rock stars, but surprisingly not many people do it. As discussed in Chapter 6, we must have true humility, and this means that we do not think we are better than anybody else. That is why no matter whom you encounter make sure to treat them like a rock star, and if that is hard in some situations, at least make sure you are always treating others as decent human beings. Being able to hone this ability is not a suggestion; it is a must for achieving success with others in your life, and because so many people don't do this you will really stand out from the crowd.

Second, address people by the name they want you to call them. There is nothing that shows others that you actually care about them like remembering their name, and for such a little thing it can make such a big impact. People love hearing their name, and in a lot of ways it is a representation of who they are, which is why it is so important to them. Additionally, for people whose names aren't easy to pronounce or people say them wrong all the time, by taking the time to actually try and learn their name you really show them how much you care, and when people know you care they want to care about you.

An exercise where you can work on remembering names is by reading someone's name tag somewhere like a supermarket, restaurant, etc. and trying to call them by their name the entire time you are together without looking at the name tag again. At first you may forget, but scenarios like that are very low risk and very high reward. Ultimately, the secret is you need to find a system for remembering names and working until you have the correct pronunciations because they will make a big difference in making people feel important.

2. Be an active Listener. Although listening was addressed a little bit in Chapter 6,, active listening for the purposes of this chapter is a little different. Active listening is a combination of knowing how to best listen to others, being interested not interesting, and knowing what to say and when to say it. I am going to address a few items under each of each of those areas, but there is one overarching theme to realize about active listening — you need to give 100% of your attention to the other person. Don't be on your phone, don't be directing your attention to other places, and don't be focusing on what you are trying to say next instead of what they have to say. We all need to realize that listening is more than hearing the words someone else is saying. It is being able to comprehend and understand what the person just said so you can move forward in a conversation. Not only will you save time because you won't be asking over and over again for them to repeat themselves, but people can tell when you are really paying attention, so building relationships will become easier in the process because people

gain a sense of trust when they feel like they are actually being listened to.

When it comes to knowing how to best listen to others there are two rules I try to follow. The first is giving people time to answer. As someone who is used to talking because of my career, sometimes I have to make sure I am not violating this rule, and that is why I wait to give thirty seconds before continuing to ask other questions or talk again. For some of us this can seem like an eternity, but not only does it show that you care for them enough to wait for them to figure out what they want to say, but because they have been given the time to form out a well-formulated response you know it will be worth it.

The second rule is don't interrupt or say anything until you are sure the other person is done talking. I had to work on this personally for a long time before getting where I am today with it, but every time you interrupt someone who is talking you are being rude, and unless that is how you want to be known and ultimately push others away, it is really important to not interrupt.

Building and maintaining relationships requires you to show care and interest in others, and no matter how interesting, important, or life changing what you have to say is, just don't say it in the middle of someone else speaking. Additionally, if you are thinking about what you want to say in your head before the other person is even done talking then obviously you aren't listening.

In addition to knowing how to best listen to others, you also need to be interested, not interesting. By showing a sincere interest in what others have to say, you will win their hearts over instantly because you are showing them what is important to them is also important to you. Two ways to do this are by getting others to talk more than you do and being interested in what they talk about. First, you want to make sure they are talking more than you are talking. Many times people don't want to hear what you have to say, but they just want someone to listen so by giving them that opportunity you are making them feel like you are interested in how they feel, and that is important in any relationship. Also, if you want to gauge who is dominating most of the conversation just think in your head that the goal you want to strive for is a four to one ratio. For every four minutes of talking they do, you want to make sure that you are doing no more than one minute of the talking. Keeping this in mind can help you measure whether or not you are talking more than you should, and eventually you will want to bring the one down as low as possible so all you are doing is speaking to guide the conversation while you are listening to what the other person has to say.

The second way to practice active listening is by showing a sincere interest in what someone else is interested in. Although you may not want to talk about something, building relationships isn't about what you want, it is about doing what someone else wants, and eventually you will form a relationship where your interests are mutual. Sometimes as individuals we need to take that first step to show we care and by valuing what they are interested in return they begin to value us. When they value us in return the relationship will start to grow rapidly, and if that is the ultimate goal then we need to be willing to put in the effort to get to that point.

The last way to be an active listener is by knowing what to say and when to say it. First, think about what you are going to say before you say it. I am sure someone has told you this before because I know I have heard it in my life more than once, but even though we hear it we don't do it. By taking the time to think about what we are going to say before we say it we can make sure that what we are about to say next isn't harmful, isn't unnecessary, and isn't going to make us look like a fool in front of the people we want to get to know better. Too many times we end up in these situations, and all we had to do was think about what we were going to say before we actually said it.

The second area of interest is not talking every time you feel like talking. Although we always think that we have the best one liner, the piece of information that will save the day, or the best idea since sliced bread, we will actually get farther with others by letting them do most of the talking. This can be difficult in conversations where there are elevated emotions, but it is in these moments you want to keep your mouth shut the most because you are more than likely going to say something you are going to regret. These things can ruin relationships that already exist or prevent new ones from ever forming, and by following the simple saying my grandma always tells me, we can make sure we never experience that regret: "The best things ever said were left unsaid."

3. Handle arguments. As you are putting yourself out there more to build relationships, eventually you are going to come across some discourse. Even the best communicators make mistakes sometimes, and if they are the masters then it is almost assured that people like you and me are going to encounter these situations. The good news is there are ways to handle these conflicts, and I want to share my tips with you so you can handle arguments in your own life.

First, let sleeping dogs lie. The biggest way to handle arguments is by preventing them in the first place. You can do this by avoiding them when they come about and by not actively seeking them out. But not all discourse is bad and not all of it can be avoided in our lives. Sometimes discourse is necessary to bring out the best ideas to move forward and be successful as a group, but knowing how to best handle these situations is key if you want arguments to be fruitful and not destructive.

Second, understand other's perspective before making assumptions. It is important in any situation that you use your skill of active listening to figure out exactly what the other person is thinking, why they are thinking it, and what outcome they are seeking through the discourse. Once you understand their perspective you are much more inclined to have a fruitful discussion, and not push each other away. Just because you don't agree with another's position doesn't mean you can't respect it, and by showing you understand and respect the way they see the situation you create a mutual understanding, which allows for relationships to stay strong even if you have disagreements.

Third, remember being right isn't always right. Although we need to first understand the other person's point of view in an argument, we also have to be willing to determine if us being correct is more important than making the other person feel like they are right, which will strengthen your relationship with them. People can be right all the time, but when you look at how much they accomplish and the amount of strong relationships they have in their lives, there tend to be very few or none at all. There is technically no winner in an argument where someone has to end up being on top because someone will ultimately be humiliated and as a result most likely strike back in anger later on.

Fourth, seek the best possible outcome for all parties in an argument. When in an argument you need to be able to weigh everything going on in order to seek the best outcome for everybody involved. The best outcomes normally involve a little give and take until the best possible resolution can arise. Take the initiative to understand what the other person wants the most and what you want the most, and then while keeping those two things in mind suggest a solution that will benefit everybody. If a solution like that can't come about then make sure not to push a solution because that will do more damage to relationships than good. If a solution does seem like it is possible, get the other person to think that it was their solution because not only will they feel more inclined to support what they believe was their idea, but they will respect you more for agreeing with the solution they proposed. It shouldn't matter who gets the credit if everyone gets what he or she wants.

The last tip addresses situations when you get in an argument with someone who is full of anger or beside themselves. These situations are never pretty, but like arguments, you are bound to find yourself in one at some point in your life. The first thing you can do in these situations is not fight fire with fire. By getting angry with someone who is already upset, you aren't going to get anywhere. Instead of lowering yourself to their level, which is in most cases what they want, take the high road. Second, don't fuel the fire, douse it with water. Sometimes it is our natural inclination to allow things to burn out of control, but we have the power in our hands to douse water on the situation as well. By staying calm, speaking softly, and killing the other person with kindness, the situation can be deescalated most of the time. Just be careful because if you did something to make the other person angry, this method could come off a little condescending. Third, act completely contrary to what the person expects you to do. For example, if they say you are a bad person then say yes thank you for noticing. Although you need to be careful, by acting contrary you will begin to damper the fire because they aren't getting the response they want. Also, once they have calmed down from there fit of rage, really do something they don't expect by being kind to them, praising them, etc. The last thing someone expects after they yell at you is to be treated kindly. It may sound wild, but if the goal of the situation is the let the other person express their feelings so you can move on and build a relationship in the future, then by acting contrary to what they think you most likely will be able to achieve both of those goals.

Building and maintaining relationships is all about communicating effectively with others. To start mastering this skill always remember to make others feel important, be an active listener, and handle arguments appropriately. By implementing all three of these skills you can be assured that you will be able to build new relationships, strengthen old relationships, and work with others to achieve the best outcomes, and now that you can build relationships, you now need to learn who you should be forming those relationships with.

Surrounding Yourself with the Right People

Throughout history no one ever achieved anything of significance without surrounding themselves with the right people. Essentially that message is what this section is about, and until you can effectively surround yourself with the right people, the ability to achieve whatever you want in life may still be out of reach. The good news is I have some techniques for making sure the people you surround yourself with are going to help you in your journey for success in the face of adversity, and they all focus on building your support network.

Before getting into why you need a strong support network and how to construct that network, there is one fact that you should know first — you are the average of who you surround yourself with. As Jim Rohn put it "You are the average of the five people you spend the most time with." Knowing what you know now, take some time to reflect on this concept, and think about the people in your life that you spend the most time with. After that think about the five people who you would spend the most time with if you could. These are important things to start asking yourself, and when you are constructing your support network they will help you in deciding what type of people you should be associating with.

There are many reasons why we need support networks in our lives, but when it comes to succeeding in the face of adversity none seem more relevant than having people help pick you up when you are struggling to do it on your own. I know my mom is a key member of my support network, and without her support throughout my journey I could still be on the ground telling myself life isn't worth living anymore. These people are crucial to have in your life, and although we should be strong enough to stand on our own like the last chapter suggests, we need to realize that sometimes that won't be enough.

There are just some things we can't do on our own as well as we can with others. That is why successful people know they need to surround themselves with people who are stronger than them in their life. In addition to picking us back up when we can't seem to do it on our own, people in your support network also function in other ways that ultimately result in our ability to grow and become stronger. First, they can provide us with a fresh perspective in our lives. Sometimes we are too immersed in what we are doing or too close to the situation to see it clearly, so your support network can help you out by providing an objective point of view. Second, people in your support network can provide you with feedback. As mentioned in the last chapter, criticism can do a lot of harm if not handled the right way, but when the closest people in your life are able to provide feedback to help you grow then you are more likely to accept it and become stronger. Third, they can hold us accountable. The people in our support network should know what we want to achieve in life the most, and in addition to helping us reach that goal, they can also help us by making sure we are doing the things we set out to do in order to be successful.

Now that you have an idea of how a strong support network can make you or break you, let's discuss the types of people you should include in your support network, and what traits they should exhibit. There are four types of people I think worth including in your support network — family, friends, coaches, and mentors. Although each type of person has a different perspective they bring to the table, in a lot of ways their roles overlap. Before I get into why you need these kinds of people in your life, let's discuss some of the traits these people should exhibit before letting them get too close.

When determining whom you would want to have as coaches and mentors in your life, their level of achievement and ability to do what you want to do are important factors to look into. But the bottom line is that any one of the four types of people you let in your support network should have certain characteristics, and if they don't then you probably shouldn't be surrounding yourself with them. A lot of these will be familiar because they are the traits you look to develop in yourself to strive to become your best, but there are a few differences.

First, people in your support network should be honest. Although honesty can be tough to swallow sometimes and the truth may hurt, you want people in your life who are going to tell you how it is. Success doesn't come from being pampered and told what we want to hear, and without having people in your life who are willing and able to do this you will have trouble succeeding. Also, if they lie, cheat, steal or anything else that is not honest, chances are they aren't looking out for your wellbeing.

Second, people in your support network should be loyal. People who are loyal have your back, and no matter what situation arises in your life they will continue to do so regardless. Fair weather friends are not the type of people you want to associate yourself with because when you need them most they are gone.

Third, people in your support network should have your best interest at heart. This is a harder trait to judge at first because people in your support network must be honest and loyal in order to have your best interest at heart. Having your best interest at heart doesn't mean that the people in your support network are going to drop everything they are doing in their lives to help you succeed at the expense of their own success, but what it does mean is they want to see you succeed, and if there is anything they can do to help you achieve that goal, they will. Sometimes people are only concerned about themselves, and if it came down to them achieving success at your expense then they would do it in a heartbeat, and that is why making sure the people in your support network have your best interest at heart is so crucial.

Fourth, people in your support network should be positive. Although the next chapter will address positivity more in depth, the important thing to understand is that you don't want to surround yourself with negative people. Negative people can drag you down, make you lose confidence in yourself, and limit your chances of achieving success in your life. But even worse, in those situations where you need their positivity the most they won't be there. Sometimes we all need a pick-me-up in our lives, and if the people in your support network cannot provide that positive attitude and bring you down from their negativity, then you want to make sure they are nowhere close to you when constructing your support network.

Keeping these traits in mind, I want to first discuss family and friends as people you want to have in your support network. Family and friends are some of the most important people in your life because they are the ones you spend the most time with. Although coaches and mentors may shift into becoming family or friends, they have distinct roles, as you will read in this section. Additionally, due to the amount of time family and friends spend with you, they are also the people who

107

know you the best. That makes them specially equipped to help you in your life to succeed.

Family and friends are normally the people you turn to first when something of significance happens in your life. This could be something positive like wanting to share your latest achievement with them, or this could be something negative like a severe medical diagnosis. Either way we are drawn to these people, so it is important that they exhibit the traits laid out in the previous section because these people have the influence to help or hurt these big life moments.

Family and friends are also the people most likely in our lives to pick us up when we need it. If they have honesty, loyalty, and keep our best interest at heart, they tend to be able to help us get back up on our feet where we can get back in control.

Family and friends also offer unconditional love. Although having the title of family and friends doesn't ensure these people will have unconditional love towards you, if these people are in your support network it should almost be a requirement. They know the good, the bad, and the ugly, and despite having some negative interactions here or there, in the end you both love each other and want to see each other succeed, and it is this feature that truly sets family and friends in your support network from all others in it.

Having a better idea of why family and friends are distinct from coaches and mentors, I now want to describe the roles these latter types of people play in your lives. The saying goes "For anything you want in life there is a relationship that can get you there faster," and in this case these relationships are coaches and mentors. Coaches and mentors are anyone who can provide you with insight, advice, wisdom, or help you achieve success in your life. They are the people in your support network that don't just provide emotional support, but also what you need in your life to achieve whatever you set out for because they have been there or done it already.

As discussed earlier, one additional trait that you need to assess when determining who the coaches and mentors you want to have is their level of ability and achievement. You want to be sure that they have not only had success in the area you want them to help you grow in, but also still have the ability to have success again. The reason for this is because the idea of having a coach or mentor is to learn from their experience to be successful, and if they don't have that experience then they won't be able to help you in the way they are supposed to. Although our own personal experience is important in our growth, other's experience is even more valuable. By using what coaches and mentors have already experienced in their life, the trial and error process to learn what they know almost goes away completely, and you won't need to make the same mistakes to get to the level of success they have been able to achieve in their lives.

When it comes to coaches, the distinction between mentors is that they don't necessarily have the ability to do the thing that you want to be able to do in your life, but they have the ability to help you get to that point, which is where their value lies. Think about sports. Most of the best coaches in the world aren't necessarily the same as the superstars they coach, but they have the ability to help those superstars hone their skills to become their best, and that is what coaches do in your life. They encourage, guide, and develop the performance of someone who is seeking to achieve high levels of achievement.

Mentors on the other hand are people who have already achieved success in the same area we want to achieve success in, and can provide us their personal experience about what it took to get to where they are. They are interested in helping you achieve success, and that doesn't mean always building you up and making you feel good if you don't deserve it. Although mentors aren't cruel people, they are not there to work with people who aren't willing to push themselves and get a little uncomfortable in their pursuit of success. If they are successful, chances are a lot of people want to have them in their support networks, so you must be ready to do what they say. If they hold all the characteristics listed earlier in this section at heart, then even when they are being harsh, they are just being honest and telling what you need to do. Plus, nothing is greater than having someone who is successful acknowledge your accomplishments. By having strong mentors in your life you have a source of motivation, because you not only want their respect, but you also don't want to let them down.

Overall, surrounding yourself with the right people will make the greatest difference in the level of success you are able to achieve, so make sure when constructing your support network that you are putting in the time and effort that it deserves. By using the skills from the first section on building and maintaining relationships, make sure once you have these relationships in place that you cherish them because if they are the thing that could make or break you then you should treat them with that level of importance. Nobody wants people in their life who just take, take, take, so following the Golden Rule don't act in a way you wouldn't want to be treated.

Living a life of service

Building relationships and surrounding yourself with the right people are game changers in people's ability to succeed in the face of adversity. But if there were one thing to take away from this chapter, or honestly this entire book, it would be this concept of living a life of service. Living a life of service has completely changed my life, and if a life of fulfillment is what you are seeking then this is a non-negotiable. There is a difference between success and true success, and if you want to experience the success that will make you happy and fulfilled in your life then you need to get out of the mindset of what can I do for myself, and get in the mindset of what can I do for others.

Sadly there are people in this world who believe serving others, giving to others, and helping others is only something suckers do, but these people don't realize how much they lose by not giving. While there are many benefits to giving to others, like the sense of fulfillment that accompanies it, those aren't the reason you should live a life of service. The reason you should choose to live your life this way is because it is the right thing to do, and most importantly when you succeed with others you succeed in life.

For the rest of this section I want to talk about what a life of service looks like, why we should choose to live this way, and the ways that our actions can come back to benefit us in countless, unforeseen ways. Living a life of service isn't something you can get others to do by telling them to do it, but is something you get others to do by wanting to do it. Although it has been a little tricky to come up with how to get people interested in themselves to become interested in others, I have found the best thing we can do is live by example. By showing others through our actions how we are making difference in others' lives and how everyone is better off as a result, we can gradually shift their perspective of being self-centered and switch to being community-centered.

Being community-centered to me is when you make your decisions in the mindset of not what will benefit or harm you personally, but what impact it will have on others. That is because community-centered people know when more people are successful we are all more successful, and realize the simple truth that they wouldn't be where they are today if it weren't for so many people who contributed to that success. As John Donne wrote "No man is an island." One of the reasons why people should live a life of service is because in many ways they should feel obligated to. None of us got to where we are today without the great inventions people developed throughout history, the great battles fought to protect the rights and freedoms that we have, and the things people have done in their lives that have somehow benefited us in a way we will never know. People who say they got to where they are on their own are terribly misinformed. Knowing so many people have contributed to our success, how can we not feel some sort of moral obligation to do the same for others?

In addition to being community-centered in your thoughts and actions, there are many things we can do as

111

involved members of our communities whether they are as small as the town you live in or as big as the community of the entire planet. All of these things stem from generosity, and they aren't what people should have to do, but what people should want to do. First, you can live a service-oriented life by helping people accomplish tasks in their own lives without expecting anything in return. Sometimes all people need is a helping hand to make a big difference and, who knows, your hand could be the one they need to do it. Second, be loyal to those who have helped you get to where you are in your life. There are so many individuals, groups, and organizations that have helped you succeed, and just because you have experienced success doesn't mean you should turn your back on them now. In reality, you should want to support them the most now because you know the impact they can have on people's lives and you are living proof of that. Third, there are more ways to help people than just financially, so whether it is performing manual labor, standing in solidarity with others, or just providing support and encouragement to the people who are working to make everybody better off as a whole, realize that whatever you do to help others makes a difference. The moral of the story is just give whatever you can, because by giving you will ultimately receive some of the greatest gifts you can ever receive in life.

Although the things you receive from giving to others should not be the reason for doing them, here are some of the tangible benefits you receive from helping others and living a life of service. First, you will receive a sense of happiness and fulfillment like nothing you have ever experienced before. People who aren't willing to give are always lacking satisfaction in their life and are always seeking more in their quest to be happy, so if you want to be happy in your life then it is time to stop thinking *what can I do for myself and start thinking what can I do for others*. Second, people will have a sense of admiration and appreciation of you that can't come from any other source. Although there are lots of ways to build relationships and how to make them stronger, the bond formed when you are giving freely to help others rather than focusing on your own selfish desires is something that can't be rivaled any other way. Third, and probably the most important of all, is the way in which your service will come back to benefit you in ways you never could have imagined. Although the story I include at the end of this chapter will delve into this benefit in more detail, know that what you do today by paying it forward could be one of the biggest differences in your life down the road. Although there is no way to measure it, those who give will always get more back in return, and if you don't believe me then start giving and see just where it gets you.

Living a life of service is the one thing in your life that will bring it from good to great, and from unfulfilled to fulfilled. In addition, you will help others succeed in their lives and you can feel the self-satisfaction that you are doing everything in your power to succeed like many people did for you in your life. Changing the world is honestly possible if we do it one person at a time, and I believe that we can move mountains if we move them together, so by working as a community instead of individuals the things that will be possible together will shock us all.

Summary

You finally have reached it to base camp on our climb up the mountain, and that is something you should be proud of. By communicating effectively with others, surrounding yourself with the right people, and living a life of service, your success should no longer be hindered by your ability to incorporate others in your life. Not only will you be able to achieve success, but with the relationships, support networks, and communities behind you to succeed, no adversity will stand in your way. To sum up the top lessons in this chapter I included a list of the 10 most valuable points, and after them is a personal story of how I applied this principle in my life to be successful.

Tim's Top 10: Incorporate Others in Your Life

1. Succeeding with others is succeeding in life

2. Make others feel special by treating them like a rock star and remembering their name

3. Actively listen by letting people respond, being interested not interesting, and knowing what to say and when to say it

4. Handle arguments by avoiding them, understanding others points of view, and not fueling the fire

5. Being right isn't always right if your goal is to make friends and not push them away

6. Surround yourself with a strong group of people who can support you in your life

7. Cherish the people in your life that support you by doing more for them in return

8. Be community-conscious and make decisions with others best interests at heart

9. Help others achieve success in their lives without expecting anything in return

10. Remember all of the people who played a role in getting you to where you are today

Principles in Action

There are so many moments in my life I could share with you where embracing this principle has contributed to my success, but I feel there is only one story that does it justice and captures the magic that can come from incorporating others in your life – the story of how my amazing community of Fulton New York came together to save my life. By sharing their story I feel I can let them know how much they mean to my family, so they will never think we forgot what they did for us when we needed it most. I also mentioned earlier how you never know how what you do for others will come back to impact you, so after hearing this story I hope you can start to see the true value that can come from living a life of service and paying it forward.

Throughout my childhood my parents were always very involved in my community. Both having worked in education, my parents wanted to not only foster a strong community within their schools, but outside of them as well. My father instilled these values as a physical education teacher in the Fulton City School district and as the head coach for the varsity football and wrestling teams. Our community rallied around football and wrestling, and although I always sort of saw my dad as a legend in my community, he never could have done it without my amazing mother by his side. Not only was she the coach's wife who provided a support network for the coaches, players, and my brother and I, she also changed the lives of thousands of students in my community as a kindergarten teacher, elementary school principal, and district administrator. Although my dad might be the "legend," I think my mother is the true hero, and I can't imagine anyone exemplifying more in my life what it means to serve others without ever expecting anything in return than her.

Throughout my childhood my parents emphasized the importance of treating others with respect, doing what was better for everyone rather than me, and paying it forward by helping others. As a result I did many things in my life like helping my parents organize Respect Day in our community, attending different events such as our community's American Cancer Society's Relay for Life, and being the water boy for the football team. What I didn't realize at the time was how my parents were teaching me one of the most valuable lessons of life, which is living a life of service. But at the same time they would actually be laying the groundwork for what would end up saving my life in the future, without any of us realizing.

After getting sick, there wasn't much to propel me forward in my life, but before I arrived home from my multiple day stay in the hospital, everything my family had done for our community was about to pay off greater than any one of us could have imagined. In just a few weeks my house was stacked from one end to the other with foods and goodies sent by people who had found out about my illness. There were toys to keep me busy, like a new PS3 and iPad I received, and food ranging from cookies to casseroles to pizzas to barbecue. If someone believed we were missing something, it would show up in the blink of an eye. My friend Hannah's mom Geri had to actually start scheduling when people would bring things like food to our house because the support we were getting was almost out of control. In addition, my mother helped me start a caringbridge.org page to post about my journey to keep people updated with the latest news, and before I knew it classmates, community members, and people I didn't even know were sending me prayers and words of encouragement on the website.

Although this was all amazing and my family and I thought we were getting back more than we had ever invested in our community, when my cancer relapsed and I lost my sight, my community just fought harder to do more even while my own body seemed to give up. They would rally together to do more than my family ever could have asked, and this culminated in one of the greatest community benefits ever. I don't know if they realized it, but together my community ended up raising tens of thousands of dollars to help my family pay for costs that would pile up fast from traveling back and forth to Boston, and without it I am not sure how my parents could have kept up with the costs of travel, lodging, and medical bills – all with more zeros than my mother would like to ever see in her life again.

I will never be able to thank my community enough for what it has done for me, and I continue today to pay it forward and help others because whether it is me again or somebody else, there will always be someone who needs that support in their lives, and without it they may no longer be here today. My mother's iconic phrase is "It takes a village to raise a Tim," and although I may not be able to ever repay all the people in my life for what they have done, just like perfection you never stop striving for it, and when it could be the difference in saving someone's life there is nothing I would rather do or could make me more fulfilled in my life than doing it.

Chapter 9 View the World Optimistically

Viewing the world optimistically is the second to last principle we need to address in our journey towards a life full of success in the face of adversity. The last of the five ALIVE principles is *Experience the Life You Want To Live*, and in order to get the most out of it you will need to be able to master the three skills in this chapter and view the world optimistically.

The three skills taught in this chapter are radiating positivity, being gracious and appreciative, and having hope and faith. They are all about having a positive outlook on life, and the benefits that accompany them are not only personal, but beneficial for others as well.

Although it is sad to realize, many people make a choice to view the world through a negative lens, and as a result it causes them pain and suffering. It also brings down the people closest to them, and eventually can push them away. Sometimes this negativity can be a part of our circumstances, but I have learned through my own experiences there is always a bright side to every situation, something to be grateful for, and always a light at the end of the tunnel if we are willing to look hard enough for it.

To help you understand the role *View the World Optimistically* plays in your life, we should look at the mountain climbing analogy again. So far we have made it to base camp by making the decision to learn about everything you need to know, making yourself as strong as possible, and building up a team of supportive and successful individuals. These three steps together have gotten you to base camp and the first part of summiting the mountain is complete. The next step now is starting your trek up the mountain. To start the trek up the mountain you will need to embrace a positive mindset, remember how grateful you really are, and have unwavering belief that you will accomplish your goal. That is what viewing the world optimistically is all about, and here are the skills so you can start trekking up the mountains in your own life.

Radiating Positivity

Every time something happens in our life we have two choices. One is respond positively. The other is respond negatively. Radiating positivity is not only making the choice to respond positively no matter what happens in our lives, but it also involves having a positive attitude that brings everyone around us up as well. Like most things in our life, a positive attitude is a choice, and that is why I am going to share with you the benefits of a positive attitude and how to be more positive in your life. And how you can radiate that positivity to others.

Think about that person in your life that you enjoy being around because they are so positive. It seems like no matter what happens they are always enthusiastic, happy, and as a result bringing up the people around them. Our goal in life should be to strive to become just like them, and then we will start to see the benefits of positivity for ourselves. And since positivity is a choice, anyone can do it. It may not be as easy for some as it is for others, but through being disciplined as we discussed in Chapter 7, eventually you will be able to get there.

The three largest benefits of having a positive attitude are having the power to conquer adversity in your life, being able to stay calm in stressful situations, and attracting others to you. First, people with the ability to always look on the bright side of any situation can conquer any adversity in their life. People who are successful realize this, and they know it takes a positive attitude to achieve positive results. As Zig Ziglar said, "Your attitude, not your aptitude, will determine your altitude."

Second, people with positive attitudes don't get overwhelmed easily in stressful situations. They realize that situations seem much worse in the moment than they actually are, so instead of reacting negatively they stay composed so they can act the way they need to in order to mitigate the issue.

Third, people are attracted to positive people. Like the name of this section suggests, positivity is something that is radiated, and by having a positive attitude you will bring up others in your life. Positivity is also contagious, so like a chain reaction other people who are influenced by your positivity will then be able to radiate it on to others themselves, and as a result everyone will be happier and more fulfilled. It is important to remember that positivity and negativity cannot occupy your mind at the same time, so by mastering the thoughts that occupy your mind through discipline, negative thoughts will have a much more difficult time trying to enter it. Knowing this, the next paragraphs will include ways to maintain and radiate a positive attitude so you can start doing them in your life like I do in order to practice becoming a master at it.

1. Look at your adversity in a positive light. Although it may be tough if you are currently experiencing serious adversity in your life, being able to look at your adversity in a positive light not only takes away power from your circumstances, but it gives you the power to become stronger. Think of it like digging for nuggets of gold. There is a lot of crud you need to sort through in order to get to the valuable pieces of what you are digging through, but if you dig far enough you can find them. My theory in life is that if you can't find something positive about your circumstances, then you just aren't trying hard enough.

I always say that in a lot of ways it took me having cancer and losing my sight in order to gain my vision. Although some people think that is a little much, I truly believe that you can harness your adversity in your life to make it better, and like failure can be a learning experience, adversity can be turned into optimism and success. Although I wish nothing bad upon anyone ever, sometimes I think we all need some adversity in our lives because there isn't quite anything like it to help you shape yourself into the person you are meant to be. No one promised us life would be easy, but we have all the opportunities to be successful despite that.

Again, I want to emphasize that this was not always the way I saw my cancer experience and blindness, and it is just what I learned over time. I struggled, I was pretty negative at times, and I didn't want to listen to what others had to say because they didn't understand, but now I want to let others know that taking this mindset towards adversity in our lives is the best thing we can do, and ultimately I hope you don't need to go through all the trials and tribulations I faced in order to learn this powerful life lesson.

2. Control what we can control. Too many times in our life we try to control circumstances when it is impossible to do so. Although it would be great if we could, some things are just out of our hands. What is in our hands is how we respond to these uncontrollable things. Having a positive attitude relies heavily on this belief, and that is why throughout the book I have emphasized the point that the power to control the outcomes in our life are in our hands. Successful people understand this universal truth, and realize that it isn't what happens to them but how they choose to respond to it that counts.

Two of the things we can control in our lives are how we feel and what we are going to let bother us. First, imagine every day that you had the chance to wake up and assign a number 1 through 10 on how great your day was going to be. What number would you pick? Was it a 10? If not, why? I just gave you the option to set how great of a day you were going to have, and if you picked anything but a 10 then you directly influenced how well your day is going to be by setting the bar lower than what you could have chosen. How we feel is a self-fulfilling prophecy, and if we say that we are going to have a less than perfect day than that is what will eventually manifest, but if we say we are going to have a perfect day then chances are that will manifest itself into reality as well. That is why it is important to realize that we have the power to control how we feel, and when we start exerting what we can control we can make large differences in our lives.

We also have control over what we let bother us. Nobody else can tell us what is going to upset us and what isn't, so that responsibility solely rests in our hands. Of course, there are always going to be those things in our lives that drive us nuts, but by knowing what these things are we have direct control on how we are going to react when they do happen. That is the overarching theme here, and instead of worrying about what we can't control, let's do the things we can to reach the highest levels of success in our lives.

3. Think in terms of solutions not problems. We all have that friend in our life that radiates positivity that we want to be around all the time, but there is also that person in our life that radiates negativity and tends to bring us down. One of the biggest differences between the two people is in their view of whether the glass is half full of half empty, but even more importantly whether they are focused on solutions or problems. Having a positive attitude means that you focus on solutions, best possible outcomes, and the reasons why things can work instead of thinking of all the problems in your way or why it will never work. Not only will others be more attracted to the solution-based person, but you will find that your ability to achieve timely success in your life will increase as well when you aren't focused on all of the problems and negativity that could happen and most likely won't: "Any fool can find fault, but it takes a winner to find solutions." (Launching a Leadership Revolution by Chris Brady and Orrin Woodward).

4. Look at things as possible not impossible. Too many times before people even try to accomplish something they have already accepted it isn't possible. This way of thinking is the opposite of what having a positive attitude entails, and the worst thing is most of the time we are the ones who put these limitations on ourselves. As the name of this book implies, success in the face of adversity is when we push the notion of what we perceive as possible because the power to define what that means is in our hands. Throughout history people have gone on to do what is supposedly impossible again and again, so why should we believe that there is an invisible wall that will prevent us.

One example that really hits home for me is Roger Bannister's triumph over the four-minute mile. Until he accomplished this feat in 1954 everybody said it was impossible. Instead of giving up Bannister kept working harder and harder,

121

and eventually he would go on to do the so called impossible by running a mile in less than four minutes. Also, after he broke the four-minute mile, others have gone on now to accomplish this feat, and it just goes to show once people can see it is possible for themselves then they feel like they can actually do it. Have a positive attitude towards what you can make possible in your life, and by working hard to change what is perceived as possible there won't be much adversity that can stand in your way.

5. Remember it only takes one person to make a difference. A lot of people think because you are just one person you can't make an impact in the world, but that couldn't be farther from the truth. Even though it is important to remember nothing great was ever achieved by someone on his or her own, every great vision, mission, or idea was first brainstormed in someone's mind. From there that individual began spreading their message, until it resulted in the change they desired to see in the world. Change happens one person at a time, and if you can ever change one person's life then you need to remember that you already have changed the world. It only takes one person to spark a massive flame, and with the right attitude that person could be you.

6. Encourage others to be their best. As mentioned in the last point nothing great was ever achieved by someone on their own, and the best way to get the most out of the people around you is by encouraging them. Encouraging others can bring the people around you up, and as a result they are more willing and able to accomplish more. By radiating your positivity to others, eventually that radiation will come back to benefit you and boost your morale, so being encouraging not only benefits others, but yourself as well.

When attempting to encourage others, it's also important to remember you have no idea what is going on in a person's life at any given time. They could be having the worst day in the world, and by encouraging them you could make the difference between them wanting to give up and continuing on. You never know the last time that person heard anything encouraging from someone else in their life, so never leave it up to chance and encourage others to succeed.

7. See the best in people. Although you can't be naïve by letting people take advantage of you or possibly hurt you, we all need to start looking at the best in people more by having a positive attitude toward others. Positive people look at people as decent human beings who wouldn't go out of their way to hurt someone for no reason at all, and as a result they are more trusting and don't push away others because of differences. Instead, they choose to embrace others by believing everyone shares the common trait of being human. As a result the people you are surrounded by don't live in fear of one another, but instead in love and admiration. In a world where it seems all the media portrays is the negative and bad in the world over and over again it can make it very difficult to find the good. But this just means that we need to fight our fears and see the best in others more than ever. The next time you see someone don't think of how they could be bad, and think how they could be good because 99.9% of the time that is what they are regardless of what the media would have you think.

8. Don't hold on to your negative feelings, and forgive. What many people don't know about forgiveness is that it doesn't hurt others as badly as it hurts you to not forgive them. Only good or bad thoughts can exist in the mind at one time, so by holding on to anger, a grudge, or seeking payback, negative thoughts will never fully rid the mind. Remember, forgiving someone doesn't mean that you forget what someone has done, but it means you are not going to let their actions cause you pain anymore, and you shouldn't be burdening that pain if you had nothing to do with it anyways. Just think during the next time you are struggling with this that it isn't your job to judge others, and know that eventually they will have their day.

9. Brighten the world with your smile. Smiling is a cornerstone of positivity, and it makes you and others feel better, so it is a requirement for anybody who plans on developing a positive attitude and radiating positivity. If you want to test the personal benefits of smiling the next time you are upset, just do

it. Although there is a science behind it, basically when we smile we trick our brain into thinking we are happy, and as a result we actually become happy. Additionally, smiling can brighten other people's days and foster a positive environment where everyone is able to be more successful, so the next time you see someone that doesn't appear to be having a good day, greet them with a warm and inviting smile. For something that can make a big difference in your lives and others' lives, smiles are free, so smile every time you possibly can because the results will shock you.

10. Laugh every chance you get. Out of this list I would honestly place this point as the most important for having a positive attitude, and that is because it helped me beat cancer, it helped me overcome my blindness, and it has helped me in the different times in my life when I just needed a pick me up. People have called laughter the best medicine for a reason, and that is because it works. In addition to laughter being contagious and making a room brighten up instantly, it can help you in situations that seem like in the moment the worst thing in the world.

Perhaps people believe I am just a little goofy, because I always laugh at my life even in scenarios where most people would be crying. For example, one day my guide dog Lang pooped in the middle of a hallway at my school because he didn't want to use the bathroom when we were out in the rain. At that point I had a choice to make, and although I was not happy, frustrated, and a little embarrassed, I had the power to choose how I would respond to the situation, and I chose to laugh. Nothing can diffuse the situation, make you feel better, or put things back in perspective like laughing can, and if you want to overcome adversity in your life and be successful learn to laugh because you can't receive the benefits you get from doing it anywhere else. Besides we can't fuss in our life every time a little thing like our dog pooping inside happens, so choose to live life and just laugh.

By taking all of these points to heart, you now have the mindset, tips, and skills to have a positive attitude, and, ultimately, radiate positivity. The benefits to yourself and others are numerous, and a lot of these points are simple and easy to incorporate in your life, so don't wait, and start becoming that person others think of when they think of the positive person they know in their life.

Being Gracious and Appreciative

This section on graciousness and appreciation will focus on achieving true happiness in your life. True happiness is a result of feeling internally grateful for everything you have, and by externally expressing those feelings through appreciation towards others who have helped you achieve what you are grateful for. By learning how to think about what you have rather than what you don't and remembering that everything you have in life you wouldn't have if it weren't for the help of others, we can feel a sense of fulfillment in our lives that will translate over to feeling blessed.

When it comes to being happy in your life honestly how would you rate it on a scale of 1 to 10? If it's not a 10 why do you think that is? Chances are none of us are at a 10, and that's because we aren't as gracious and appreciative as we should be. By being gracious and appreciative we should be satisfied with what we are blessed to have in our lives, and want to share that feeling with the people who provided those things. Viewing the world this way is an antidote to unhappiness, and without being happy in our lives all of the success we are able to achieve won't mean much because we will always want more.

Graciousness is a feeling of gratitude for everything you have in your life that others may not have in theirs. Instead of focusing on what you don't have that others do, you focus internally on what you do have. Gracious people are happier with less because they value what they do have so much more, and people always have something in their life to be grateful for even if that is just having the opportunity to experience another day on this earth.

As far as adversity is found in our life, people who are truly gracious realize there is always a reason to be grateful, even if we don't know what those reasons are in that moment. Accompanying this idea is the fact that no matter how much we have to be ungrateful for in our lives, there will always be more to be grateful for. Learning this lesson has completely changed my life, and I believe it can change yours as well.

Every time I struggle, get in a tough situation, or think could things get any worse, I take the time to remember when I was in the hospital with little hope of survival because that was the darkest moment of my life. Although a little extreme, this is my way of telling myself whatever I am dealing with at any point in my life now isn't that bad, and that fills me with the motivation I need to continue on to succeed. It's important to note sometimes thinking of how far I have come isn't strong enough on its own to motivate me, so I take it one step further and think of all of the children who are experiencing what I went through right now. By thinking of how hard they are fighting I can again fill myself with the strength I need to push on because it's not just about me, it's about all the people worse off than me right now.

Now that you know the benefits of a grateful heart and having a gracious spirit, here is a technique on how you can strive to become more gracious in your life. It involves being grateful every day for what you have, and being able to draw upon that feeling of being blessed when you need it most. You can do this by writing a list of everything you are grateful for, and although it is simple it can make a big difference in realizing just how blessed you really are.

There are three steps involved with making a gratitude list. First, spend ten minutes every week writing down everything you are grateful for in your life. Don't worry if you can't get everything down, and focus on the larger areas in your life then gradually include the tinier and more specific areas where you feel blessed. The important thing is that you are reflecting on what you are grateful for, so make sure to make this a part of your schedule every week.

Second, after writing the list, take five minutes to think about the people who contributed to achieving those things in your life. Although you probably played a big role in those achievements, nothing we ever accomplish is possible without the efforts of others in our lives, so we need to think hard about who these people are. In these five minutes, write the names of individuals, groups, and organizations next to the item you are thankful for which they helped you achieve. After multiple weeks of doing this you will have a full list of things you are grateful for in your life and who helped you to get them, and then comes the most important piece of creating a gratitude list.

Third, look at one item on your gratitude list every day. Don't just look at it, reflect and think of why you are just so grateful for what you wrote down, and how grateful you are for the people who contributed to it. By performing this action every day you will become more gracious for everything you have in your life, and eventually it won't matter how much others have because you realize you already have so much.

Although being gracious creates an internal sense of blessing that can help you persevere through the adversity you face in your life, by outwardly appreciating others you can share your gratitude with everyone else. That way, you can constantly remind yourself how others play an important role in everything you have in your life. This helps prevent you from becoming arrogant and reminds you why living a life of service is so important. At the same time you are building others up and letting them know you actually notice them and the generosity they have shown you. By doing this you encourage them to repeat the action again and it makes these people feel good inside, which will ultimately strengthen your relationship with them.

Out of all the ways you can express your appreciation for others, I don't think there is any stronger method than by doing one of the simplest and most impactful things in the world... saying thank you. We should all get in the habit of saying "Thank you" at least once a day to someone, and it could make a huge difference in how you feel about yourself, and about how people feel about you as well.

One of the biggest things to remember about appreciation is that it has to be sincere. As my parents said when I was younger, "Don't say sorry unless you mean it," and in keeping with that same logic, don't say thank you unless you mean it. By saying thank you, you acknowledge the fact that someone has done something special for you in your life and your thank you should reflect just how special it was. This is also a great way to remember all of the people who helped you, even if it was years ago. In many ways it is more important to make sure that you aren't taking the people for granted who helped you get to the current point in your life. By forgetting where you came from you cannot only ruin a lot of relationships, but you can also cut your foundation out from underneath you so when you need to rely on those people in the future they won't be there.

Another tool I want to give you to use in your life is actually writing down and sharing with others how much you appreciate them, by writing a thank you letter, preferably a hand written one. A thank you letter not only shows someone how much you care, but how much you were willing to put in to make them feel extra special. Again this is something simple, but the truth is not a lot of people do it.

It is important to know what a thank you letter shouldn't be before making one, and that is why I am going to explain some big red flags you want to avoid. First, a thank you letter is an actual letter. It isn't an e-mail, it isn't a quick thank you on the way out the door, and it isn't a social media post somewhere for the recipient to see it. The reason the thank you letter is so special is because unlike e-mails and other forms of messages that we receive constantly and get bogged down by, an actual letter is something we don't receive many of, which already separates it from everything else regardless of what is written inside. Second, don't sound like a robot. Be authentic, share why you are so happy for what someone did, and don't make this a thank you letter that sounds like your mother made you write it.

Here are three quick tips for writing the thank you letter, and they really can help it go from good to great. First, be timely. Don't wait to say thank you to someone because after a while it will lose its impact and seems like it was more of a last minute thought. Second, check for spelling mistakes. The worst thing you could do is spell their name wrong. Third, customize it to the individual. State what they did that made you so thankful. Let them know how what they did changed your life. And focus on creating a letter that plays to what they would receive the greatest satisfaction from.

Living a truly successful life means being happy and if you want to achieve happiness make sure to take the time to feel gracious for what you have and appreciative for how others have helped you achieved what you have. Making your gratitude list and sending out thank you letters are great starts, and like anything you do over and over again eventually it becomes a habit and this is one you won't want to try and break.

Having Hope and Faith

Viewing the world optimistically involves a positive outlook on life, and hope and faith are the means to creating this way of looking at the world. Hope is having a strong belief in something and faith is being able to hold on to that hope when it is tested the most. In order to be successful you require hope. Think back to the equation for success — hope + action = success. Hope is half the equation.

Being able to have faith and hold on to what you believe in most during the darkest moments of your life is not easy, and I questioned mine constantly with everything that happened to me at 15-years-old. But it is a discipline, and if I hadn't been able to hold on to at least a shred of hope I wouldn't be here today writing this book for you. Although the discipline of faith is not like the many other disciplines discussed in this book that have tangible ways to become stronger in it, you can work on faith by following what you believe in even when it doesn't make sense to you at the time. Because there aren't exercises I can give you to work on your faith, the rest of this section will primarily focus on the five beliefs I hold dear that have helped me become successful in my life. If you choose to believe them as well, great, but ultimately you need to decide for yourself what you believe in to be successful, and by now I trust your ability to decide for yourself what those things are.

1. Things will get better. I believe at the core of hope stands this belief. If you can have faith in this you realize that no matter how bad things get there is always going to be better times around the corner. We all will experience bad times in our life, but when it seems like we have lost everything if we can believe truly that things will get better, then we have something, and that something is hope.

2. God never gives us more than we can handle. Whether it is on my weakest days or my best days, having faith that God never gives us more than we can handle provides me with a sense of belief that I will come up on top no matter what adversity I face in my life. Also, I believe that my toughest moments aren't the end of my life, but a way to open my eyes to a new and more enlightened way of living.

While getting diagnosed with cancer, going blind, and being told I wasn't going to make it, one question I would hear a lot is "Why you?" I honestly started asking this myself, and I didn't know the answer. There were kids doing drugs, there were kids lying, cheating, and stealing, and there were kids doing things I couldn't imagine myself ever doing, but still I was the one with cancer, blind, and dying. The truth is I struggled to believe that God would never give me more than I could handle, but by somehow managing to hold onto one sliver of hope I found my answer. The problem wasn't thinking why me, but why not me. God would never give the experience I had in my life to someone who couldn't handle it, and because He knew I could endure the pain, learn the lesson He wanted to teach, and become stronger, I was able to have cancer, blindness, and almost die in my life, and still go on to succeed.

3. Everything happens for a reason. Although in our worst moments we can't see beyond what is happening to us

right then, we need to believe that everything that happens to us is for a reason, and that reason is to help us fulfill our greater purpose in life. At the time I wasn't sure what experiencing everything with cancer was actually guiding me for so my faith wavered, but eventually by never giving up my hope my answer came to me. The reason I went through everything I experienced was so I could go on to fulfill my dream in life to help others. I was always someone who was community-conscious, but by enduring my battle with cancer I gained the ability to use my story to impact people on a scale I never could have imagined before I got sick, and I believe that is my purpose in life. By losing my sight I gained my vision, and with this newfound vision I am meant to be helping others like you overcome the adversity in your lives.

4. The outcome of our life is in our hands. When everything is spiraling out of control it is hard to imagine how anything is actually in our control. My faith was tested until I learned the truth about the power I had over my life. I realized more than ever that the chance to succeed was in my hands. Life had happened to me and I was a blind cancer survivor who honestly wasn't living that bad of a life, but if I wanted to go on to be more than that then I would need to use my power to do so. Once I started truly believing I had control over the outcome of my life I had the hope to go along with my action, and from there I started achieving great things.

5. We can achieve anything we set our minds to. If we think of the five beliefs of this section as a process they would go as follows: I first needed hope that things could get better, then the hope that God never gives us more than we can handle, then the hope that everything happens for a reason, and then the hope that the power to control life is in our hands. All of this must happen before having hope that we can achieve anything we set our minds to. The hope that we can achieve anything we set our minds to is the core message of this book, and if I had to emphasize only one of these beliefs for you to take in your own life it would be this one. Believing we can accomplish what we put our minds to is a powerful thing, and *It's Impossible Until You Do It* is all about achieving what you and others might see

as impossible because you believe it can be done, and that's what matters. When you believe that something is possible you have the hope in order to achieve success, and at that point you just need to have faith in that belief to the end because that is how you bring your vision into a reality.

Summary

Viewing the world optimistically will completely change the way you live your life and how you view the world around you. It will bring you true success, it will bring others positivity and happiness, and allow you to conquer the adversity you face in your life. By taking away the three skills of radiating positivity, being gracious and appreciative, and having hope in faith you will be equipped for your mountain trek, and now all you need is the plan that will help you get to the top. But before you go on, below I summed up the top ten points in the chapter, and after them is a personal story of how I applied viewing the world optimistically in my life to be successful.

Tim's Top 10

1. Have a positive attitude where you see your adversity in a positive light, control what you can control, and see solutions not problems

2. Remember that anything is possible and it only takes one person to make a difference

3. See the good in others and encourage them to be their best

4. Be able to forgive others

5. Smile and laugh whenever you get the chance even if you don't feel like it

6. Be grateful and focus on the things you have in your life instead of what you don't

7. Keep a gratitude list that you refer to everyday to remind you of why you are so blessed

8. Show your appreciation for what others have done to you by thanking them in special ways

9. Have hope in your life by believing strongly in the things that will fill you with the strength to make it through your toughest times

10. Have unyielding faith to hold on to your hope even when you question it the most

Principles in Practice

After a whirlwind of being diagnosed with cancer, going blind, almost saying my last goodbye, going through a year in isolation, relearning to walk, and making it through my junior year of high school, I would go on to enter my senior year. But before I did, like a freshman I would be returning to the Cedar Street Practice field for pre-season practice because I was going to play football again. When it comes to viewing the world optimistically I feel this story combines all of the skills taught in this chapter, and here is how I applied them in my own life.

When I first told my doctors I wanted to play football again I didn't get the response I thought I would get, and my doctors basically said no. But eventually, after some pleading, I got them to sign my physical under the condition I wouldn't have any contact. What's football without contact, but at this point in my life I had to be gracious for the opportunity to even participate on the team again, so that is the approach I took. Things were tough for me because I wanted to be back in full force, but I kept up a positive attitude, did the activities and things I could do, even if there were very few that didn't involve contact, and through my positivity and hard work I was able to inspire my teammates to work harder and do their best. As the season progressed my coaches looked into the possibility of me snapping for extra points because the center couldn't be hit unless they made contact first, and from there I hoped that I was going to get into a game so I worked as hard as I could to master my long snap.

Although my faith was tested throughout the season because a situation never came about where I could safely make it into a game, my hope was reignited during senior night. I was already excited because every senior made it into the game on senior night, and I knew that meant me too. Sadly the game was a lot closer than it should have been, and I never was able to make it in. I was crushed, felt everything I had worked for was a waste, and almost gave up hope, but after spending a night with my teammates who I appreciated more than ever at that point, I went to practice the next morning. I didn't believe anymore that I would make it in a game at this point, but I knew I would still suit up for the last two games of the season, so I continued to work hard at practice and felt gracious for the opportunity and appreciative that the coaches had allowed me to be a member of the team.

The next thing I knew we were in our last game before the post season, and when we were down by about 30 points, my name was called with about a minute left on the clock. I didn't know what to think, and getting on the field when we hadn't scored a touchdown was not what I saw coming, but it's what happened. The other team had agreed not to hit me, and I got out to not only play three plays, but I played in the position I played before I got sick—center. I did three shotgun snaps that were better than my average with my sight. I believed that somehow, even when I didn't think it was possible, I could succeed in the face of adversity by setting my mind to it—and I did. Not only did I succeed, but I was recognized by New York State with an award for my positivity and ability to bring up my team even though I couldn't actually do it on the field. Let my experience be a lesson in what can happen if you view the world optimistically, and always believe you can achieve whatever you set your mind to because you never know until you do it.

Chapter 10 Experience the Life You Want To Live

With four principles down I am excited to say that you have now reached the fifth and final principle, *Experience the Life You Want To Live*. This principle is where the real magic occurs because it is where you bring everything together that you have learned so far, and apply it towards your goal of living a successful and fulfilling life. Like all the principles, understanding *Experience the Life You Want To Live* will require diligence, discipline, and determination, but in the end it will be worth it. We no longer need to let our circumstances determine the outcomes of our life, we no longer need to let the bad things that happen in our life keep us from living the time we have left, and we no longer have to believe what we want to achieve is impossible because that power is in our hands.

The final three stills taught in this book are setting goals, getting your priorities straight, and succeeding in the face of adversity. They are the recipe for achieving your dreams, reaching for the stars, and bringing your vision into a reality. Also, they are the last pieces you require in your life to go from living with limits to living without limitations.

Some people say they can't do it, some people say it is too hard, and some people will tell you they are doing everything possible to achieve success in their life. I am here to tell you we can no longer limit our lives by these and many more excuses. These excuses only hurt us. If we use excuses then we are the ones who don't accomplish anything in our lives, not the other way around. With the skills offered in this chapter you won't need excuses because you will have the tools *to Experience the Life You Want To Live* in the face of any adversity in your life.

When it comes to the mountain climbing analogy, so far we have reached base camp by adventuring outside of your comfort zone, living in alignment with who we are, and incorporating others in our life. After reaching base camp we started our trek up the mountain by viewing the world optimistically, and now we are at the last step to conquering the mountain. That step is summiting. Summiting the mountain will involve vision, prioritization, and the ability to overcome any barriers we experience along the way, but in the end the result is standing at the top of the mountain. Experiencing the life you want to live is what it means to conquer the mountains in your life, and I am excited to provide you now with the skills that will help you bring your dreams into a reality.

Setting Goals

In order to achieve success in any area of your life, you will need to learn how to set goals. They are the key to actually achieving the success you desire rather than just talking about it, and they have three parts. First, create a vision. Second, define the goals that accompany your vision. Third, make a game plan to execute your goals in order to bring your vision into a reality. Together these three steps work wonders, and combined they are the formula for bringing your dreams into a reality.

1. Vision. When it comes to goal setting the first thing you need to do is have a clear vision of what you want to accomplish. There are three reasons why you need to have one before you go on to define your goals and create your game plan. First, whatever picture you can create in your mind you can achieve. As the saying goes if you can see it you can be it, and until you can clearly see what you want to achieve you won't be able to bring it into reality. Second, your vision is your motivation. When you have your goals set and use your game plan to execute them, chances are you will run into some problems that aren't in the master plan. In these moments you need to be able to refer back to your vision in order to remember why you were so passionate in doing what you wanted to achieve in the first place, and that motivation will help you continue on to bring what you want into a reality. Third, your vision is the destination that you base your goals on. Without having a clear destination of where you want to be you can't clearly define the goals you need to accomplish to get there. So without a vision your goals will be all over the place leading you somewhere, but you have no idea where that actually is.

Now that we have a better idea of why we need a vision first, I want to now give you the steps so you can form a vision of your own. First, find somewhere quiet where you can think. The goal is to find a place where you feel comfortable to gather your thoughts and not get distracted by your surroundings, so whatever that place is for you, head there. Second, once you have found your quiet spot sit for fifteen minutes and really think about all the things you want to achieve in your life. What are you doing, who are you with, and why is this what is making you so happy are some of the questions that you can ask yourself to get your brain working, and then let yourself form that picture in your head. Third, when you are done get your thoughts down on paper. It could be a drawing, words on paper, etc. but the goal is to get what is in your head out onto paper so you can use your vision to help you define your goals to bring what you put on paper into a reality.

2. Goals. Once you have created your vision you need to work on defining your goals. Your vision is only a wish if you don't take the time to define the goals required to bring it into a reality, so don't think your job is done yet. In this step you need to make sure you not only set your goals, but you also do it the right way because a bad goal will only give you false hope. In order to make sure you don't fall into the trap of coming up with bad goals, I have included a list of eight criteria your goals should meet in order to make sure they are worth it.

Criteria for successful goals

1. Goals must be written down. Like your vision, if you don't write it down there is no way to go back to it, and on your journey of bringing your vision into a reality you are constantly going to want to recheck what you need to do to get there to make sure you are doing what you need to.

2. Goals must be clearly spelled out. There can be no guess to what your goal means, so you can't just put something like becoming healthy. What you could put down though is that you want to lose fifteen pounds, which will make you healthier, but is also something specific you can now strive for.

137

3. Goals must be made in alignment with who you are. In Chapter 7 you learned about yourself, what you value, and what you stand for, so when you create your goals you shouldn't compromise that. Goals that contradict with who you are as a person will eventually fail, so solve that problem by addressing it right of the bat.

4. Goals should be realistic. Although you should still shoot for the stars, don't make your first goals your final destination. Set yourself up for success, and accomplish small goals which will eventually give you the confidence and ability to take on the big goals because you can achieve whatever you put your mind to.

5. Goals need a date for completion. If you don't set an end date for when you are going to accomplish your goal then you are giving yourself way too much room to not ever get it done. For example, if you know you need to complete 100 pushups before noon everyday it might provide you with an incentive to start early to make sure you get them done without putting strain on your body.

6. Goals should be written as if you have already completed them. By writing your goals as if you did them instead of you are going to do them then they are more likely to bring themselves into a reality because you have already put down somewhere that it happened. Also, make sure to read them out loud twice a day because talking as if you have completed them will also translate over eventually into them coming true. For example I climbed Mount Kilimanjaro versus I am or will climb Mount Kilimanjaro.

7. Goals need to stay at the forefront of your thoughts. Wherever you go you should always have your goals with you. They can guide you in making decisions, remind yourself what you need to do to be successful, and provide you with that extra kick in the butt when you are thinking about doing something that would be contrary to them.

8. Goals shouldn't change. Although your game plan that lays out how or when you are going to accomplish your goal may change, the actual goal itself shouldn't ever change.

Using this list you can be sure that your goals will have a high success rate when it comes to how strong they are. Now you just need to create your game plan.

3. Game plan. At this point you have your vision, you have the goals you need to accomplish to bring that vision into a reality, and now you need the game plan to be able to execute it. Although this can sometimes be the hardest part because you aren't 100% sure what you need to do and you feel like no one has ever done something quite like what you are trying to do before, you need to embrace the skills from Chapter 6 here. Don't let your lack of knowledge and fear of failure prevent you from forming your plan to get to where you want to be, and if you need a little hint here then copy genius. Chances are even if your goals and vision are different from what you think anyone else has ever done you are exaggerating a little bit, and you need to find the people who have succeeded in accomplishing something like you are setting out to do and learn from them. These people probably made mistakes along the way like you will most likely as well, but by learning what they did you at least won't have to make the same mistakes they did, and as a result you can possibly do what they did even faster.

Because your goals won't change but your game plan will. One way to write out how to achieve your goals and game plan together is by writing your goals in pen and your game plan in pencil. By writing out your goals and game plan this way you can symbolize things that won't ever change, and things that may change depending on how effective they are. Also, unlike goals which are singular in nature, chances are the steps you will need to take to achieve them will be more than one, so make sure you give yourself some room to write down all the pieces required in your game plan to achieve your goal.

When it comes too actually writing out your game plan there isn't really a model or criteria I can provide you with to be successful, but the important thing is that you write down what you think you will need to accomplish your goal, and be willing to change when you learn how to accomplish what you want more efficiently. As you move closer and closer to your goal the steps you need to take will become clearer, and eventually by following your game plan you will reach your destination, accomplish your goal, and bring your vision into a reality. If the fear of the unknown is really holding you back in developing your game plan, just remember you know a lot more than you think you know. If your goal is to lose weight you know not to eat bad food; if your goal is to do better in school you know to study more; and if your goal is to be a better athlete you know you need to practice more. A lot of the time it isn't the lack of knowledge, it is the lack of drive, so take what you have learned here and be ready to use it in order to achieve success in your life because you now have a strategy for successfully setting your goals at your fingertips.

Getting Your Priorities Straight

In order to get your priorities straight you first need to know how to manage your time, you then need to be able to prioritize what is most important in your life, and then you have to focus on actually doing what you need to do in order to achieve success in your life. Combining these three methods for getting things done as efficiently as possible with the goals you set in the last chapter will create the best system for completing your goals.

An inability to manage your time, prioritize, and focus can contribute to feeling like your life is out of your control, which is why mastering these methods of getting your priorities straight are so crucial. If you have ever felt like you are working hard but it doesn't matter than these are three areas in your life that you need to pay attention to. You need to work smart not hard, and if you are able to put in less hours, but put more into those hours to be just as successful wouldn't you do it? I know I have, and when you do the same I'll let the results in your life speak for themselves.

1 Time management. Time is an enemy we all face in our lives. We all only have so much of it, it goes by slow when we want it to pass, and it goes by too quickly when we want it to drag on forever. Although we can't change those feelings or guarantee how much time we have left in our lives, we do have the power to manage our time, and when you manage your time well it feels sometimes like you control it.

How many times have you heard "I don't have time to do this" in your life? For me it is more times than I can count on my fingers and toes, and that is just from all the times it has come out of my own mouth. The truth is, we always have time and when we say we don't what we are really saying is that we don't care and don't want to put time into it. Although that isn't a bad thing and will be discussed more in the priorities section because knowing what you can and can't do in your life is important in achieving success, this section has a different focus.

What this section primarily is going to focus on is how to get the most out of your time and how there is actually a lot more time in your day if you know how to structure it right. The best way to illustrate this is to use a time-tested analogy I have found for showing people how they can fit more than they think is possible into their days. I encounter this analogy over and over again whenever I am learning more about time management, so I am not going to try and reinvent the wheel here. Instead I will take my own advice and copy genius.

We'll discuss the analogy about rocks in a bucket. Imagine a bucket is empty that represents all of the time you have in your day, and we can fill it with as much as possible as long is it doesn't overflow. The items we can place in the bucket are big rocks, smaller rocks, pebbles, sand, and water. How would you fill the bucket? What would you put in first? Could you get it all to fit?

After taking the time to think about it, if you thought about putting anything but the biggest rocks in first than I have to let you know that you need to start thinking a little differently. What you need to do to get everything to fit in the bucket is to go from the biggest items, which are the large rocks, to the smallest and easiest to fit items, which is the water, because eventually you will fill the bucket to the brim with no more room for anything else to fit in your day if you do it right. By starting with the big rocks, which wouldn't fit in the bucket if you put smaller rocks in first, you then pour the smaller rocks over them. Because the big rocks have a lot of space between them, the smaller rocks are able to find spots where they fit. From there you pour in the pebbles, which squeeze between the big rocks and the small rocks, and eventually continue the process until the sand and water have completely filled the bucket to the brim. Essentially this is the way you need to think about managing your time, and if you don't start with your big rocks or important things you need to get done first than you will never be able to fit them all in, which is why people can work hard and in reality not get a lot done because they aren't working smart. In addition to not working smart, sometimes when we are managing our time we just have more things than we could place in the bucket even if we fit it all in the right way. When you run into this issue you need to start prioritizing and deciding what needs to stay and what needs to go.

2. Priorities. Having a better idea of how we can now fit more into our days, we need to determine what we are actually going to fit in the limited amount of room in the day that we have left, or else we end up never completing everything we planned. One way to do this is by limiting the number of goals we are trying to accomplish in our life. We really should only focus on two to three goals at a time, but many times people are trying to succeed in so many different areas that they could have as many as ten goals they are working on at one time. Having too many goals is a recipe for disaster, and the best way to limit the amount of goals is by going back to your vision. Determine what the things are that you need to accomplish, and then pick the two or three biggest to focus on. Once you complete one you can replace it with another, but until you cap the amount of goals you are working on you will never find the time to succeed at any of them.

Another way we can determine what we need to be working on in our life is through assessing who we are and determining what is most important to us. If there are things that you enjoy doing in your life then don't try to do so much that you can't find time for them. You will become upset because you aren't getting to do the things that make you happy in your life, and when faced with the choice of doing something you have to do and something you want to do, you'll choose the latter. Time management is about alignment, and although some people will tell you to balance your time, you should be putting your time and effort into the areas you need to improve on, get things accomplished, and what you enjoy most to maximize your time instead of trying to balance among things that ultimately won't be sustainable, so you will need to find other areas to cut from that aren't at your core.

One way to determine what these areas we can cut away from are is by going through are day in our head and thinking about the things we do that are fun, but are in reality a waste of time. Do you surf the web, do you spend countless hours watching the same negative news over and over again, or do you watch videos on YouTube to pass the time? While although these things can be amusing, if you want to optimize your time and achieve the most you can as possible towards achieving the success you really want in life they are going to have to go.

Although those are good strategies for determining what we should include in our day and sorting out what really isn't important to us, one more tip to maximizing the time you have in your schedule is by learning to say no. We do a lot of things people ask of us even when those things will make it harder for us to be successful, so by limiting what we add on top of our busy schedules we can accomplish more, and eventually be able to do more things in our life that we enjoy because we have accomplished the tasks we need to get done. One important thing to note is that things like relationships and serving others although may not seem important or fit in your vision or goals the way you think they will, but remembering what you learned in Chapter 8 such as succeeding with others is succeeding in life and no one ever accomplished anything great on their own, you need to make sure you include room for them because they are just as important for your success and do not necessarily fall into this category of saying no.

3. Focus. Once you have determined the things you need to do in your life the last thing is focusing on getting them done. Chances are we are going to have more than one thing we need to accomplish in a single day, so knowing how to put your rocks in your bucket in the right order now comes into effect. The important thing to highlight here is no matter what you do, make sure that you only take on one task at a time, and don't continue on until you have completed it.

A way to think about focus is by thinking about the sun's rays. By the time they hit the earth most of the power they have that could have incinerated us has dissipated, and that is what it is like to have a lack of focus. Your energy becomes dissipated, and you are unable to do much with it. If you took a magnifying glass though to the sun's rays and refocused that energy on particular spot than you would have enough energy to melt little toy soldiers and incinerate ants. Not that those things are cool, but the idea is by focusing all of your energy on one thing at a time you can accomplish it as fast as possible.

In today's age where it is almost impossible not to find people multi-tasking, this principle just reinforces the need to focus on one thing at a time. You will be able to accomplish a lot more doing things one at a time then doing multiple things at the same time. Also, when you accomplish a task you feel good because you have actually accomplished something, and you can do even more with that boost of energy from each success.

Another aspect to focus is creating an environment that you can work in. You need to limit the distractions wherever and whenever you decide to work on something, and by doing so you will get tasks done faster. This working environment should be somewhere where you aren't forced to think about having to do other things because a wandering mind is just as harmful as external distractions.

Finally, the best way to optimize the time you have in your day is by biting the bullet and taking on the biggest and most important thing you need to accomplish that day first. By getting that big task complete first you not only feel a great sense of satisfaction, but you then have a lot of time left in your day to do the little things and the things you want to do. Also, if you wait to do the biggest or most important thing later in the day you run the risk that you won't finish it on time, so getting that thing done right away just makes a lot of sense.

By understanding how to manage your time, how to prioritize, and how to focus to maximize what you are able to accomplish in a given day you can effectively and efficiently get everything you need to done. Applying these methods to your goals will result in your ability to accomplish goals like you never have before. Ultimately, you can have all of the tools to succeed, but if you can't succeed when you are confronted with adversity in your life than you aren't equipped yet to experience the life that you want to live.

Succeeding in the Face of Adversity

Succeeding in the face of adversity is the last skill that you will be taught in this book, and in a lot of ways I was saving the best for last. Although I have highlighted other skills like living a life of service and having hope and faith, your ability to succeed in the face of adversity is what we've been working towards this whole time. The three areas you will need to master in order to succeed in the face of adversity are fueling your inner fire, staying persistent towards what you want in life, and ultimately what this book is all about, the ability to persevere.

First, you need to be able to keep your inner fire burning strong at all times. To me our inner fire is our drive, motivation, and passion to want to succeed, and without it a lot of bad things can happen. You can lose hope, you can lose self-confidence, you can push others away, and the list goes on. We all need to have our purpose and drive for what we want to achieve in life, and I have found three ways to do this.

145

One way is to stop and smell the roses. *It's Impossible Until You Do It* is about the process not the destination, and if we are too concerned about the next step we need to complete then we will start to diminish our inner fire. Instead, we need to look at how far we have come, and celebrate all of the little successes we have along the way. These celebrations will refresh us and show us we are making progress, and like accomplishing any task it fuels you with more energy to go work on the next one.

A second way is to constantly remind yourself why you are doing what you want. If we want to succeed in the face of adversity we really have to want it bad, and constantly reminding ourselves how bad we want it and why we are doing what we are doing in the first place will keep our inner fire going. The ins and outs of the things you need to do every day can sometimes wear on us, and it is where this reminder is needed the most to make sure we keep our inner fire burning bright.

The third way is to put yourself on the line. There is nothing that can ignite your drive to succeed like knowing if you don't it means you are going to lose so much, so when you are taking on your adversity put it all out there. Don't hold anything back, don't give yourself the room to back out when things get tough, and don't let negativity sneak its way into your head.

The second area you need to master is persistence. Persistence can be summed up by doing the hard work no one else is willing to do, without putting up a fight because you realize the importance of it. Persistent people practice constantly to become their best. Persistent people don't complain. Persistent people don't make excuses. Persistent people just keep working until they have accomplished what they want to achieve.

Having an idea of what persistence is, there are four ways you can make sure that you are striving to be persistent in the pursuit of what you want in life. First, keep your inner fire burning. The more you want to achieve something, the harder you are willing to work and do the things you don't necessarily want to but need to in order to be successful, so by keeping your inner fire burning you allow for yourself to be persistent.

Second, have your goals handy. Knowing what you need to do can provide you with the constant reminder of what it takes to achieve what you want, and seeing them on paper is the best reminder. Third, view the world optimistically. You need to stay positive in the journey for success in the face of adversity, and when things feel like they may be too much you have to remind yourself of everything you know about being positive, gracious, appreciative, and full of hope with faith to back it up. Fourth, surround yourself with the right people, and hopefully you have people in your support network that can hold you accountable and encourage you to continue to have persistence in your life.

In addition to these four ways of keeping up your ability to be persistent, there is one more thing I want to share with you about persistence. At times you are going to feel like you have just had enough and that is when your persistent attitude is most important. Successful people will tell you that triumph came only one step after they felt like giving up the most, so as bad as things may get keep pushing forward because success is right around the corner.

The third and final thing you need to master to succeed in the face of adversity is perseverance. Perseverance is one of my core values, and no matter what people call it, it is the one thing that will separate people who will succeed in the face of their adversity and the people who won't.

In a lot of ways perseverance isn't something that can be taught, it isn't something that can be practiced, and it isn't something that can be honed. Perseverance is what comes when you say "I am tired of being pushed around," and you are not going to let it happen anymore.

Although this book includes a lot of knowledge that you can apply to your life to be successful, when you start putting these principles into action everything isn't going to be perfect. Things are going to come up, all heck is going to break loose, and just when you think things are looking up, you may here from someone you love "You have cancer," like I did.

147

In these moments we have two options. To lie there and take the punches, or to stand back up and fight back against our adversity. Although the latter is much tougher, it is what will result in the most satisfaction in your life, and the biggest secret to succeeding in the face of adversity is one that has been preached through this whole book. The power to control our lives is in our hands, and keeping that belief in mind and having hope that we can accomplish anything we can set our minds to nothing can stand in our way.

Perseverance isn't hope and it isn't a mindset. It is an active choice to choose how you are going to live your life, and that life is where *It's Impossible Until You Do It.*

Summary

With everything you've learned in this chapter combined with everything you have learned throughout the book there is no doubt in my mind you can Experience the Life You Want To Live. By setting goals, getting your priorities straight, and succeeding in the face of adversity what happens to you should no longer determine what you are able to accomplish. You no longer need excuses, you no longer need to feel out of control, and you no longer need to stand by and let life happen to you. All you need to do is actually do it, and before I leave you with my closing thoughts below are my top 10 most valuable points from this chapter and how I have applied this principle to my own life.

Tim's Top 10: Experience the Life You Want To Live

1. Form a vision in your mind of what you want to achieve and where you want to be in life

2. Set goals that will set you up for success

3. Create a game plan with steps on how you are going to accomplish your goals

4. Work smart not hard by putting in less hours but putting more into those hours

148

5. Determine what the most important things are in your life that you need to do to get what you want and say no too everything else that doesn't help you get there

6. Focus on one task at a time removing all other distractions from your life when you are working

7. Complete the biggest task you need to accomplish in your day first

8. Keep your inner fire burning strong for what you want in life

9. Have a persistent attitude where you constantly work towards what you want in life

10. Persevere through any barriers that stand in the way of what you want in life

Principles in Practice

One story really stands out to me where I embraced the principle of experiencing the life you want to live and that story is how this book ended up becoming a reality. It all started off with a vision, and although it didn't get me very far because it wasn't a good one, it is where the seed was planted to write a book about my experiences. After going through so much in my life, and somehow managing to continue living and working hard to succeed, people told me all the time I should write a book. I talked about it a lot, I thought it was a good idea, but that was five years ago. I didn't have any goals, I didn't have any game plan, and I barely even had a vision. Eventually, in 2015 I took what I had learned in my life about accomplishing what I wanted, and I decided I didn't want my book to be talk anymore. I was going to do it.

From there I had to take my vague vision of writing a book and determine what exactly that book was going to be about. It took me a couple of months to really get to the core of this, but I needed to accomplish this goal before I could go on to other ones like actually writing the book. I knew I wanted to include my story of overcoming cancer; I knew I wanted to include information people could apply to their lives that I learned firsthand worked; And I knew I wanted most of all to create something that was going to help people all over the world in their lives so they could overcome their own challenges.

From there I no longer had a vision problem, I had goals set to achieve what I wanted, and a game plan of what I thought I would need to do to get there. The problem I did have was a priority one. I didn't put much time into my book, the every day of school consumed my life, and before I knew it I had basically cast something aside that was important to me. It wasn't until the beginning of 2016 that I realized I needed to make my book a priority if I was going to get it done, and from there I started devoting more time to it, cut out things from my life that weren't going to help me achieve my goal like clubs and activities on campus, and focus on getting something done every week to move forward with it.

Eventually I was making headway with my book, but then I would need to really embrace the skill of achieving success in the face of adversity. I had to fuel my inner fire to stay motivated, I had to be persistent, and most importantly persevere when life took its unexpected turns. Probably the biggest turn for me was setting a date to get the book done by December 10, but I would end up getting sick and being out of commission for two weeks, which threw everything off. This is where all of the principles in my life came together to make this book possible. I adventured outside of my comfort zone by putting my credibility on the line to get this book out on time regardless of the fear I was facing. I lived in alignment with who I was by pushing myself to succeed and stay confident when doubt seemed to be creeping in from every angle. I incorporated others in my life by leaning on my support network to help me finish everything on time. And I viewed the world optimistically and had hope that everything was going to work out. As a combination of everything taught in this principle, which relies on what was taught in the other principles as well, I was able to succeed in the face of adversity, and ultimately summited the mountain I have been talking about all book.

Conclusion

Life isn't about the destination; it's about the journey. Throughout the book I have provided a mountain climbing analogy and although your destination was always to get to the top of the mountain, it means nothing without everything you had to do to get to that moment. That is why you always need to keep in mind that the secret to a fulfilling life isn't just the quick moments where you can say you achieved something you set out to do, but it comes from enjoying every moment along the way on your path to get there. Also, as I have learned firsthand and from mentors in my life, the top is only the halfway point. You only succeed after you have gotten back down safely, and in my analogy this means that once you achieve something you want in life that doesn't mean it is over. We can always do more and become stronger, and although perfection isn't possible we will get a lot closer to it by striving to hit that point than if we accept we can't ever get there.

At the beginning of this book I made you a promise. That promise was if you take away even one thing from this book you will feel more in control of the outcomes in your life than ever before. I hope I fulfilled my promise. I also hope you were able to take away more than just one thing from this book to aid you in your journey of success in the face of adversity.

It's Impossible Until You Do It isn't a fad, the hottest trend, or something you do. It is the way you choose to live your life, and it means you can achieve anything you want in life in the face of your adversity regardless of what others say. The only one who can place limitations on ourselves is us, so as long as we believe we can do something don't let others tell you otherwise and what you can and can't do.

One of the concepts I have mentioned again and again throughout this book is that knowledge is powerful, but it doesn't mean anything unless you actually apply it. Don't just look at this book and think I know what to do now to be successful. Actually put these principles into action, or else you will just have hope. Hope without action only results in a lot of

152

talk, big dreams, and things you want to do, but in the end that is all it is because you never do anything to bring the vision you believe so much in to a reality.

I don't want you to live a life of talk, big dreams that never come true, and never getting the chance to do what you want. What I want for you is a life of success and fulfillment and I know that is only possible through action. I believe that the principles in this book can provide you with what you need to have that action in your life, but again you are going to have to take that first step. I wish I could take it for you, but at some point in all of our lives we need to make the decision whether we are going to let life happen to us, or happen to it.

Although I may not know you I would like to think that we have formed a bond through the pages of this book, and in my heart I know you can do it. Whatever that it is, I know if you set your mind to it that you can accomplish it. That is why this book is called *It's Impossible Until You Do It*. For me at different points in my life that was walking again without leg braces graduating from high school on time, and getting this book published. Although those examples are what it were to me, you have your own it in your life, and just remember whatever that it is will be impossible until you do it.

We all have the power in our hands to succeed in the face of adversity. The question is and always will be will we use that power even when things get tough to get what we want. Although I see a brighter future, I can't predict it, but that doesn't mean I can't have hope. I know you have what it takes to succeed, and the only one who will ever stand between you and what you want in your life is yourself.

As I learned at a young age we are never guaranteed another day on this earth, and keeping that in mind if you aren't going to start achieving what you want in life now… when? Everything you want will remain impossible in your life until you do it, and with that knowledge take that first step so you can start succeeding in the face of adversity.

Want More?

"America's Ambassador of Hope," Tim Conners is a sightless visionary who will change the way you look at the world. His battle with cancer, losing his sight at 15 years old and his mission to live life fully, make a difference, and redefine possible have uniquely positioned him as someone who has the ability to create real change for the people he speaks to. Taking all of the life lessons he has learned throughout his journey about succeeding in the face of adversity, Tim has created a proven system to help anybody overcome the adversity in their life so they can experience a fulfilling life of their own.

Although there are many motivators in the world, there is only one Ambassador of Hope, and this ambassador has dedicated his life to serving others. He believes "Regardless of the challenges you face in your life, you have what it takes to succeed. It starts by awaking the vision within you."

Interested in having Tim Conners come and speak to you and your group?

Send him a request by submitting your information on his website MounTimPossible.com

With all of his adventuring, changing lives, and service endeavors Tim's schedule fills up fast, so if you want to have one of the best upcoming speakers in the world speak to your group make sure to get your request in right away.

As a strong motivator who makes differences in people's lives, Tim can speak to your group about anything ranging from his personal story to help motivate your group to take action to any of the principles laid out in his proven system for achieving success in the face of adversity. No matter what topic you want Tim to come and speak about, you can be assured whatever you decide will be specially tailored to fit your audience and provide them with the most value he can while he is there.

Interested in contacting Tim directly?

Tim can be reached by e-mail at tim@MounTimPossible.com

Tim realizes listening is one of the strongest things a person can do, and if you want to take the time to message him he will find the time to check it out.

Interested in learning more?

Tim sends out weekly MounTimPossible Monday alerts that you can sign up to receive on his website MounTimPossible.com

He also sends out TimPossible Thursday alerts on his Tim Conners Facebook page, which you can search directly for or use the link provided on the website.

In his alerts he provides stories that will inspire, information about his latest endeavors, knowledge that you can apply in your life, and so much more. These extras include challenges that will make you stronger and get you entered to win prizes, information about the latest value adding products Tim has to offer, and limited specials and deals on what he is offering.

Interested in what Tim is doing next?

On May 22nd of 2017 Tim will be setting out on a mission he is calling MounTimPossible. Staying true to his life mission, Tim wants to live life fully, make a difference, and redefine possible. He plans to do that by hiking the highest mountain in Africa, Mount Kilimanjaro, but even more importantly he will be raising $500,000 for organizations that have personally benefited him in his life. He knows they can go on to help so many like him succeed in the face of their adversity, and he has made it his life goal to give back to all of those he knows he will never be able to fully repay for helping him get to where he is today. He hopes through his efforts people will begin to start living their lives to the fullest, he hopes his mission will make a difference for thousands of people all over the world, and he hopes that everyone will start to challenge what they think are possible for themselves and others in their life. He believes we can move mountains if we move them together, and he plans on seeing you all at the top.

Interested in becoming a part of the mission?

All of the information about the mission can be found at MounTimPossible.com including updates, information about his team, etc.

Tim realizes he can't do this great feat on his own, so if you feel you could provide something to the team, want to donate to help change people's lives around the world, or want to help him spread the word so that everyone knows about MounTimPossible he would add you to the list of people in his life he would never be able to repay.

We all have a choice in our lives to make a difference, and Tim has learned this doesn't always need to be at the level of millions of dollars.

Every little thing helps us in getting to where we want to be, and that is why no matter how small the thing someone does is, in the end those small differences from thousands of people all over the world will make one big change.

Hiking the highest Mountain in Africa, raising $500,000, and changing the way people around the world think about what is possible are not small things, but Tim does what he teaches others, and that includes embracing a mindset of It's Impossible until You Do It.

Will you join him?